AZAN

Understanding *and* Obeying *the* Voice *of* God

Jana Penland

Copyright © 2014 by Jana Penland

AZAN
Understanding and Obeying the Voice of God
by Jana Penland

Edited by Xulon Press

Printed in the United States of America

ISBN 9781498414883

All rights reserved solely by the author. The author guarantees all contents are original and do not infringe upon the legal rights of any other person or work. No part of this book may be reproduced in any form without the permission of the author. The views expressed in this book are not necessarily those of the publisher.

Unless otherwise indicated, Scripture quotations are taken from the New American Standard Bible (NASB). Copyright © 1960, 1962, 1963, 1968, 1971, 1972, 1973, 1975, 1977, 1995 by The Lockman Foundation. Used by permission. All rights reserved.

Scripture quotations taken from the English Standard Version (ESV). Copyright © 2001 by Crossway, a publishing ministry of Good News Publishers. Used by permission. All rights reserved.

Scripture quotations taken from the Amplified Bible (AMP). Copyright © 1954, 1958, 1962, 1964, 1965, 1987 by The Lockman Foundation. Used by permission. All rights reserved.

Scripture quotations taken from the New International Version (NIV). Copyright © 1973, 1978, 1984, 2011 by Biblica, Inc.™. Used by permission. All rights reserved.

www.xulonpress.com

Introduction

Thank you for reading this. I hope the greatest return on this investment is that your relationship with the Trinity becomes so real that He is known in every moment of your life. It only seems fitting to give a background of why this was put onto paper.

I grew up believing that God could speak to us, put things "on our hearts", and guide our decisions, if we opened our hearts up to Him to do so. That came from amazing parents and great churches we belonged to. Then came a period of my life that I sat under some teaching that said God doesn't speak anymore and as long as we are obeying the commands of Scripture, we are in His will. It sounded convincing. It sounded logical. I mean, we have the closed Canon after all-what more do we need? The way the Holy Spirit spoke and guided in the first century Church isn't necessary for us today. It is a different dispensation now, right?

For a long stretch my relationship with the Lord was nothing but intellectual study. Oh, I could brag on the Greek word studies I had done, I could recite where most verses came from, but I couldn't tell you what God's specific will for my life was anymore. I was just told to read my Bible, follow the commands of Scripture, then do whatever I wanted, as long as the Bible didn't state it as being sinful. God's plan for me wasn't specific, for He had given me Biblical guidelines to go by, and that was all I needed to navigate this life successfully as a Christian.

Then the Lord graciously reached down from heaven and put my future husband in my life. Deep down I knew in my heart that God was still as real as He was to Peter or Paul or Mary, I just needed a little jolt to bring that to life in me once again. So here was the opportunity! John and I didn't date very long. We (weirdly, I'll admit) spent our dates fasting and praying, trying to hear from God about whether or not we were supposed to get married (this was John's leading). Well, God *rained* His answer on us. I mean poured it down from heaven. He spoke so much and so clearly that we joked about being scared *not* to get married. That time period was my turning point.

> I will never go back. God speaks. He is real.

Since then, we have tried to seek God's will and voice on anything and everything. Issues, problems, trials, what to do that day, where He wants us, what He wants to do with our kids. "It doesn't hurt to ask" we say, yet we go through life living in shades of gray because we don't believe that to be true of our God! He spoke to people from Genesis to Revelation and we are heirs of that same intimacy. All it takes is a listening heart and willingness to obey.

1 Samuel 3 speaks of Samuel being in the temple as a young boy. God called his name (spoke to him) three times before Eli (the priest) finally recognized that *God* was the one talking to Samuel. Eli told Samuel to answer by saying, "Speak, Lord, for your servant is listening." That word "listening" is *azan* in Hebrew.

It literally and simply means: *to perceive what is being said with the intent to obey.*

That is the crux of this study. To learn to perceive God's voice so that we can obey whatever He says to us.

Happy listening. Seriously. There is no greater thrill than to connect with the God of the universe through Jesus Christ our Lord by the Holy Spirit. May we experience it for the rest of our lives and into eternity! Blessings and love.

Jana

WEEK 1
DAY 1

Do you believe that God can speak to you personally? Do you believe that you have the right, as a child of God through Jesus, to ask God questions and have Him answer you just as a good, earthly father would answer his children? I mean *specific* answers for your situation. Answers that would take the confusion out of decision-making, the mystery out of why you were created, and would give you a specific vision for your life. When God speaks about these things, and we obey them, it not only increases the fruit in His plan of redemption, but also brings us great joy to be a part of it! Does that sound amazing or perhaps scary? Not believing that God supernaturally speaks to us and intervenes in our lives could be the main reason why we have a hard time hearing Him. This study gives the Biblical evidence needed to squelch the cynical, unbelieving parts of our flesh that find faith in an engaging God hard to believe. Recall from the introduction that *azan* is defined as "perceiving God's voice with the intent to obey." We must believe He has a voice, and believe that it can be heard, before we can agree to obey it. So faith and belief are needed to azan. Another reason we tend to be "hard of hearing" is a little more personal-it has to do with how we view ourselves.

The enemy uses one other particular lie to keep us from seeking God, and if we are not careful, it works rather well. The lie says that God requires something of us before we seek Him or will be able to hear from Him. That we have to clean ourselves up, or have to be good for a certain period of time before He is ready to reconcile with us again. This is simply not true. If you have confessed with your mouth that Jesus is Lord and believed in your heart that God raised Him from the dead, you are saved. In Jesus, you are clean. You are His child. A repentant heart will be received (1 John 1:9). Daniel prayed a verse that can be used as a weapon to combat the enemy's lies of shame and condemnation.

Please read what Daniel prayed in Daniel 9:18b:

"We are not presenting our supplications before Thee on account of any merits of our own, but on account of Thy great compassion. O Lord hear! O Lord, forgive! O Lord, listen and take action! For Thine own sake, O my God, do not delay..." (NASB)

God, through Jesus, is ready to receive you. He is ready to speak to you. "Seek the Lord while He may be found; call upon Him while He is near." (Isaiah 55:6 NASB)

Jesus abolished our sin once and for all. (1 Peter 3:18) The Bible gives very simple directions to explain how to be accepted by God through Jesus in Romans 10:9, "that if you confess with your mouth Jesus as Lord and believe in your heart that God raised Him from the dead, you shall be saved." (NASB) Go boldly to the throne of grace when you have done this. (Hebrews 4:16) Believe His love for you is higher than the heavens (Psalm 108:4) and His mercy stands ready to cover your sins. Take a minute to thank Him for His mercy and grace and love. Let's just stop and ask God if there is anything in our soul that needs to be cleansed. Confess and repent, if needed; praise Him, if needed; sit and be encouraged; if needed. Let's not move until we feel as though we have allowed Him the opportunity to cleanse our hearts. Journal anything that seems to stick out to you from your time with the Lord.

Here are a couple of verses that show what it is like if God would choose to stop speaking to us.

Please read 1 Samuel 28:15. Why was Saul "greatly distressed?" (NASB)

Please read Psalm 28:1. What did David say would make his life "like those who go down to the pit?" (NASB)

Is that not amazing? I lived years of my Christian life without regularly hearing from the Lord, and I felt like I was in a pit, just like David said! Saul must have also felt this way. This "pit" is a place where we are not seeing God answer prayer or where we are not hearing His voice of encouragement and guidance. It is a "pit" where reading the Bible is just something we do without any understanding of what it specifically means for our lives-when there is no verse that "jumps off the page" as the Holy Spirit counsels us through a specific situation...this is less than the relationship that God desires. So let's look at just a few examples of what happened when people sought the Lord and heard His voice.

Please read I Chronicles 14:8-17. What happened when David inquired of the Lord's will in his immediate circumstances? Recount what David asked and what God answered.

Please read Genesis 25:21-24. What was Rebekah inquiring about? Did God answer her question?

We don't specifically know *how* God spoke to each of them, but we can see from scripture that they heard His voice and knew it was Him. They understood what He was saying-it was clear. Do you believe that God would answer your prayers as clearly? Over the next several weeks, we are going to discuss in greater detail how to train ourselves to hear Him and how to train ourselves to obey. Whether you have been hearing from Him for years, or this is brand new to you, begin with a fresh belief, and excited expectation, that He loves to hear from you and loves to speak to you, too!

What did David and Rebekah have to do to receive such insight from the Lord? (Yes, it is the obvious answer.)

Do you *believe* that God would answer you like He did them?

For examples of God speaking to people in the New Testament, please read:

Acts 9:10-18
Acts 16:6-10

Remember the time to seek the Lord is now (Psalm 32:6a)! He does and will speak to His children. We just need to incline our ear to His Spirit.

Lord, would You open our hearts and enable us to hear You clearly? In Jesus' name, amen.

WEEK 1 MEMORY VERSE:

"My sheep hear my voice, and I know them, and they follow Me"
(John 10:27, ESV).

WEEK 1
DAY 2

Prayer: we cannot hear from God without it, and He honors even the shortest prayer if it comes from a sincere heart. Pray that He will mightily reveal Himself to you today while you *azan* (perceive God's voice with the intent to obey).

Yesterday, we focused on the devastating results that happen if God chooses not to reveal Himself (or speak) to us. It is a terrible and dark place to be. The worst part is that the reason we do not hear from God is that *we have not sought Him with a listening heart*. We learned that God answers everyday, real-life prayers, and that He spoke to both men and women, both royalty and commoner. Today we are going to learn, through Scripture, that God *longs* to be known by us and *loves* to reveal Himself. We will also learn the key to unlocking that kind of intimacy with Him.

Jeremiah 33:3 (My Own Interpretation)

> Please half-heartedly seek Me. I might answer you if I feel like it that day. It will be a toss up if I listen and very likely you will just be ignored. If I do speak, it will be confusing for you to understand because I like to make you have to figure Me out. Why don't you just use your smart phone anyway? Facebook friends can tell you what job to take. I mean, really, do I have to get involved with your every decision? You really are needy. Why do you bother Me with such trivial matters? I have a whole universe to run, not just your issues. Come back later, I may have more time.

Do we not sometimes live as though this is what it says? We, of course, wouldn't claim to believe this on the surface, but we *live* this kind of disengaged, powerless prayer life and we wonder why the abundant life eludes us. We do not have because we do not ask. (James 4:2b) Not only that, we too often rush ahead and make our own decisions because we are not willing to wait on the Lord for an answer, or we just use our own intellect to make the decision because God gave us a brain, right? Yes, He did, but He wants to stretch our minds to actually comprehend His *supernatural* intervention in our lives. Lastly, we do not have answers because we do not *believe*. "God is not interested in that little thing," we think. Or, we have seen green lights from here to Zimbabwe as God works for us and we say, "Ho-hum, I just don't know if that is the Lord or not." Neither one of those thought patterns is pleasing to Him. He is after faith like a child, hearts that seek to hear from Him in every sermon, every song, every time the Bible is opened, and then *believe Him to be everything* His Word says He is.

Now look up Jeremiah 33:3 and read what it *actually* says.

Here are the original Hebrew words and definitions for the key words of this verse.

Call ~ *Qara*: to cry out, to call aloud, *to roar*
Tell ~ *Nagad*: to bring forward, to be in front, to bring to light
Know ~ *Yada*: to perceive, to understand

Now rewrite the verse in your own words with these more literal definitions in place.

This verse contains a *promise*. It is a promise from our God Who can never lie. It says that we *will* find Him. When we seek Him with all of our hearts, we will find Him. This is not a "maybe", it is a *guarantee*. Do not give up if you do not find Him today. Seek Him again tomorrow. Do not give up if you do not find Him tomorrow. He could be testing the sincerity of your heart. How bad do you want Him? If we do our part, He will always do His.

Walk away remembering and believing everything this verse says. Let's start doing it and see what *He* does. When He does show up, believe that it is Him. Please journal it in order to share with others if you feel led. Let's encourage each other with the ways that the Lord chooses to reveal Himself to us! Take the time now to go and be with Him…tell Him you are seeking Him with all your heart and that you want Him to reveal Himself to you. He will.

Oh God, I know that You will do Your part of revealing Yourself to us when we seek You with sincere, fervent hearts. Show up for us! Answer us! Move in ways we have not felt ever before or maybe for a long time. Would You do something new in our midst as we seek You? Thank You in advance for I know You will! In Jesus' name, Amen.

Week 1 Memory Verse:

"My sheep hear my voice, and I know them, and they follow Me"
(John 10:27, ESV).

WEEK 1
DAY 3

Let Him Hear You Roar!

My husband, John, was in his eigth month of unemployment. My compassionate mother-in-law gave our daughter, Abi, the gift of ballet lessons, and John was picking her up one day. My husband was hitting rock bottom with the stress of not providing for us. I praise God that he felt that way. I believe it is biblical to want to provide for your family, and I believe that through this, God was taking him to another level of seeking Him. "Seek Me with all your heart," was the phrase that John told me kept going through his head on the way there. It was as though the Lord was saying, "With *all* your heart. No more half-hearted, could yawn at any moment or lose-concentration-at-the-drop-of-a-hat kind of prayers. You want Me to really break through? Show me by *how* you pray." So my husband white-knuckled the steering wheel, looked around to make sure there was not another car close by to see him, and yelled as loud as he could for the Lord's help. He *roared*. Not *at* God, but *to* God. Within a week, he had two job offers and another interview. We found our prayers turning to, "Lord where do you want us?!" What grateful and joyful prayers those were!

Psalm 120:1: "In my trouble I cried (cried out, called aloud, roared) to the Lord, and He answered me." (NASB)

How does God want for us to seek Him? Has He revealed this to us in His word? We may have to get out of our stoic, Western mindset that says only if you are dipsy and at an NFL game can you act like what we are about to read.

Please read Mark 10:46-52.

Notice the boldness of Bartimaeus. There was no thought of the crowd, only of wanting the attention of Jesus. The scarce dignity he may have had left (after being seen as a "sinner" because of his handicap), would have been lost, but he did not seem to care. What did his outcries get him?! The very thing he sought. Look at verse 40, "Jesus stopped...and commanded that he be brought near to Him." Do we believe that our prayers, *our* prayers, would stop God in His tracks? Do we really believe this? How much we believe God loves us will show in the size of our prayers. He *loves* you. Do we ignore, set aside, or gloss over those we *love*? We might, but God loves perfectly and He doesn't. Then why do we pray as though God's love is imperfect? Why not cry out with everything we've got, believing that the Sovereign of the Universe receives our cries with an infinite love for us?

As a side note, notice that the same crowd that shushed him, glorified God when the miracle occurred. People are fickle. We seek the face of only One. We cry out for the attention of only One. And we do not cry out just *hoping* for God to show up. We cry out with the assurance from His Word that He *will*.

Please read 1 Samuel 1:9-14.

Blind Bartimaeus is yelled at for his annoying antics and Hannah is rebuked for being drunk. Interestingly, this reminds me of when mockers accused the disciples of being drunk during the Feast of Pentecost, when the Holy Spirit fell upon them in Acts 2. God wants you to seek Him with all your heart, regardless of what other people may say to you, think about you, or even if they mock you. He is worthy of being sought after that earnestly.

He is worthy of being sought after that earnestly *even if He does not allow Himself to be found*.

But who is like our God, allowing Himself to be found and promising to answer us? No one! Will it be worth it? Ask the man who was able to see for the first time in his life. Ask the woman who received a son named Samuel, who would become one of the most reknown prophets in all of Israel's history.

There are several things we are to do with all our hearts: love the Lord, serve the Lord, obey the Lord. Today is about seeking the Lord with all our hearts. We are going to have to put aside insecurity, and even be a bit undignified, if we want to catch the heart of God. It is worth it. Nothing on Earth is like His presence.

Try, just try, seeking Him with all your heart right now and see what happens. It may feel weird at first, but press in. If you have nothing "important" to seek Him about, cry out for Him alone to come, in all His fullness, to you.

I am praying with all *my* heart that you will experience Him like never before.

Father, Your Word says that You love fervent, earnest prayers from righteous people and that they accomplish much. (James 5:16-18) In Jesus You have already made us righteous, would You help us stretch ourselves to seek You harder than we ever have before? We lay aside the insecurity or timidity that would hold us back from pleasing You with a whole-hearted prayer life. Spirit, please teach us to pray as we should. In Jesus' name, Amen.

Week 1 Memory Verse:

"My sheep hear my voice, and I know them, and they follow Me" (John 10:27, ESV).

WEEK 1
DAY 4

Who Is Living My Life?

The first part of the definition of *azan* is to "perceive what is being said." This whole study is to get our hearts and minds in tune with God's voice so that we can understand that it really is Him speaking as we go through life. I wholeheartedly believe that He desires to speak to us, and that He is willing to share with us what He is doing. Next week we will dive more in-depth on how to "perceive" His voice and what it may sound like. Today's lesson focuses on the second part of that definition—with the intent to obey. No one can say that they want to obey the Lord all the time and are not tempted to ever disobey, because we still have a flesh. Our flesh does not want to obey, it wants what it wants. Putting our *willingness to obey* on the table, before we even hear from God, will tremendously help the battle with our flesh.

Please read John 5:30.

Jesus summarizes His whole life in the first sentence of this verse. What does it say?

Jesus lived His entire life in complete and constant submission to the Father. His time, His goings in and out, His healings, His teachings, His judgments. His obedience was and is always on the table for what His Father wants.

Please read Romans 8:29. What are we predestined to be conformed to?

So we *can* be like Jesus. We *can* walk in full submission to Him, filled with His Spirit and doing nothing of our own initiative. Otherwise He would not have told us to be like Him in this world. Are we going to do it perfectly? No. Even so, *seeking Him and obeying what we hear is our part, God will take it from there*.

Jesus died and rose again, sending the Holy Spirit to us so that we could have His same kind of relationship with the Father. How it must hurt Him when, after all the suffering He went through on our behalf, we do not take advantage of this life that we are now offered. It is like He is just sitting in heaven saying, "Come on, just ask! I will tell you what you need to know! Get your Bible and start praying!"

It would be a whole lot easier to do God's will if we believe that we can hear what His will is, right? How could we be told to do nothing of our own initiative if we do not have a God that speaks to us, or a Holy Spirit that lives inside of us, to guide us into all truth? How frustrating. God does not enjoy frustrating His children. He has given us everything we need to navigate this life in godliness (2 Peter 1:3).

After becoming a Christian and knowing how to hear God's voice, we now say things like, "God, I want to quit my job, but what do You want me to do?" or "God, I am really hurt by _____. What do You want me to do about it?" or "God, what do You want me to think about _____ situation?"

Who is living our lives? Us, or the Lord? Take some time to allow the Lord to search your heart and let you know how you are doing in regards to your surrender and obedience. Journal below what comes to your mind.

Is there anything in particular that you sense He is putting His finger on and wants you to obey Him in immediately? Write it below, drop this book, and go do it!

Lord, strengthen and encourage us as we seek to make Your life our very own. We will not back down because of persecution, hardship, or trial. Let those things cause us to rejoice and to find our faith even stronger than before. You have walked every road before us, and we will follow You, trusting Your love for us is great. In Your name, Jesus, Amen.

WEEK 1 MEMORY VERSE:

"My sheep hear my voice, and I know them, and they follow Me"
(John 10:27, ESV).

WEEK 1
DAY 5

There is a great mystery surrounding God's sovereignty and man's responsibility. The leadership in our church have a great saying, "God has His part, you have your part, and I have my part." How exactly that works, I have no earthly idea, but I know it is a true statement. The other day, my husband asked God, "Lord, is it okay to come to you with everything? I mean *everything* and try to hear Your voice on it?" He felt like the Lord answered him and said, "In *all* your ways acknowledge Me and I will direct your paths" (Proverbs 3:6).

These six weeks are all about training ourselves to take our questions, decisions, joys, burdens, hurts, sins, worries, praises, blessings — whatever — and hearing what God has to say to us about it. I will preface that with the fact that God is God and He does not *have* to give us *reasons* for everything, He did not with Job or Habakkuk. Still, even though God did not give a reason, He *spoke* to them in their situations! I have found it to be true in my own life that there is very little that He chooses not to speak on. What we hear may not be every detail to why God is doing what He is doing, but He will still speak.

It is exciting to hear God's direction and understand what His plan is for us. It anchors us to have a specific vision that we can hold on to and strive towards in this storm of a life. All that said, it will not be easy to live this kind of life. We may mishear Him. We may misunderstand, or be asked to do something that seems crazy to those around us. (Mind you, it will *never* contradict scripture. We will cover more on that topic a little later.) The Bible tells us that anyone who desires to live a godly life in Christ Jesus is a target for persecution. Let us look at some of the reactions people had to what Jesus did and said while here on Earth and honestly ask ourselves, "Is this worth the cost?"

Matthew 12:14: The religious authorities sought to kill Jesus.

Later in that same chapter (Matthew 12:24), Jesus was told that He was of the kingdom of Satan.

Matthew 15:10-14: The Pharisees were *offended* when Jesus rebuked them for following "tradition" rather than God's Word and His Spirit.

Most of Jesus' earthly ministry was rebuked, scoffed at, and plotted against largely by *religious people*. Moral of the story? Expect resistance to come. Expect offense to come. Do not be surprised by persecution. In fact, rejoice and bear up patiently, for there is a crown of life waiting for you (Revelation 2:10). Now does this mean that we go disrespectfully waving fists at people with our Bibles in hand and rejoice when people get angry at our unloving outbursts? No! When we humbly and confidently move forward on what we feel like the Lord is saying to us, we patiently deal with the outcome from others whatever that may be.

So, is it worth it to seek and follow God this way?

This is a valid question. Jesus did not take discipleship lightly (we will look at that more in depth in week four). In fact, if we really looked at His church-growth methods, we would hesitate to do them (well, we usually *do not* do them). He harshly rebuked the "religious" and befriended the prostitute. He forgave adulterers while threatening eternal condemnation to the ones who obeyed all the "rules." I personally have never called anyone a "son of the devil" in hopes for their conversion.

His calling is tough. It calls us to die daily, moment by moment, to His higher authority (1 Corinthians 15:31). Not only die, but to die carrying a cross. Not a pleasant picture.

His calling is the narrow way (Luke 9:23). Yet we follow Him. Yet you are doing this Bible study. As Christians we know that this life has tribulations, trials, and tears. We have experienced them. As Christians we have the distress and burden of trying to life a godly life in this ungodly world (Psalm 73). It is much easier to react to life naturally, much harder to stop our flesh and listen to the Holy Spirit instead. So what makes us see this seemingly unbalanced scale, choose the harder road, and stay on it?!

These next verses that we are going to read are fabulous. Often, they are only quoted in pieces, so here they are together.

Ephesians 3:20-21 (NASB)

"Now to Him who is able to do exceeding abundantly beyond all that we ask or think, according to the power that works within us, to Him be the glory in the church and in Christ Jesus to all generations forever and ever."

Most of the time I have heard this verse quoted it usually stops with, "Now to Him Who is able to do far more abundantly than we can ask or imagine." And that is the end of it. The question of whether or not it is worth it to seek and follow God, is not answered just in that first part, it is found in the 2nd half: "according to the power that works within us..."

*It is worth it to hear and follow God because of the **unimaginable power** that God will bring to life **in and through us** here on this earth to the glory of Christ.*

Paul is saying that God is able to do abundantly more than we could ever think to even ask or imagine *in us*. That there is a *power* and *fullness* of God we can have to the glory of Christ that we could never even dream up if we tried! This power comes when we relinquish our entire being to be filled with His love and walk listening and obeying His Spirit.

Is this kind of power the mark of your life? Why or why not? No right or wrong answer just be completely honest.

Do you believe that this kind of power is available to you? What do you think is your part in attaining it?

More about the cost....

Please read Philippians 3:8 below.

"More than that, I count all things to be loss in view of the surpassing value of *knowing Christ Jesus my Lord*, for whom I have suffered the loss of all things, and count them but rubbish so that I may gain Christ..."

That word "knowing" literally means "*experiential and intimate* knowledge of." In our Western mindset, we read this verse as mostly an intellectual endeavor. We say we know God, but then may find ourselves answering "no" to the question about supernatural power being the mark of our lives.

There are times when we have to stand on the fact that the Bible tells us so despite our emotions, but that is not where we need to consistently live out our days. We are meant, according to Philippians 3:8, to *experience* His love, to *experience* His person in and through us. Other religions desire this also and that is why they practice meditation and seek things like Nirvana. But the Christian God of the Bible wants us to meditate on *Him* and seek the power of *His* presence in us. The other ways are just satan's counterfeits for what God wants to do for us. The Bible, our plumb line of truth, just told us that we can seek to experientially know this Jesus. This love and power is not meant to be something that your mind knows and your heart never feels. Our whole being is to be supernaturally charged by the power of God in our actions and words. Those actions and words are to be authored by God through His Holy Spirit and our job is to obey them.

This seeking and knowing Christ is the only worthwhile labor to pour ourselves into both for the here and now and for eternity, so let's end our time here with a prayer telling God that, *Yes, He is worth it!*, and let's live our lives this week seeking Him as though we truly believe that!

Lord, we are so sorry for putting other things before you. There is a power waiting for us that would fulfill us far beyond what we could ever imagine and we want that power. It is the power of You living in and working through us. Would You do it in spite of us? Deep down, we are fully aware that knowing You and gaining You is the best thing we could ever experience. Please make it our reality. In Jesus' name, Amen.

Journal ways that He did abundantly more than you could ask or think *through* your life this week. How He poured Himself out *in you* as you surrendered to His Lordship, willing to hear and obey His voice over anything else.

Week 1 Memory Verse:

"The sheep that are My own hear and are listening to My voice; and I know them, and they follow Me." John 10:27 (AMP)

WEEK 2
DAY 1

Test the Spirits

Psalm 100 tells us to enter His gates with thanksgiving. Begin with thanksgiving for some of the ways the Lord has spoken to you in the past. Specifically try to recall ways that He has kept His word to you and praise Him for it. Maybe He gloriously provided for a need you had, or gave you a comforting scripture while you were going through a hard time. These things are what we must store away in our souls to remind us of His faithfulness. There may be some bitterness or anger or fear that has temporarily covered up those memories. Repent of them and replace those thoughts with thanksgiving.

This next verse makes me want to do a cartwheel (if I could) and I love the way the Amplified Bible states it.

Psalm 71:14-16 "But I will hope continually, and will praise You yet more and more. My mouth shall tell of Your righteous acts and of Your deeds of salvation all the day, for their number is more than I know. I will come in the strength and with the mighty acts of the Lord God; I will mention and praise Your righteousness, even Yours alone."

Did you catch that part about His "deeds of salvation?" What does it say about the number of them?

Why does this excite me so much? Because we tend to get in a rut of believing that once we are "saved" or forgiven for our sins and brought into the family of God, that salvation has ended! That the promise of heaven is enough. Those things would be enough and sound too good to be true! But the truth is, they are followed by acts of salvation on our behalf day in and day out if we are looking for them. Being brought into the fold of God is *one* of God's glorious works on our behalf, the crowning one, but our lives should be *filled* with testimony after testimony of His saving acts toward us! Our initial point of salvation is like the entrance to the amusement park, the beginning of the hike. It is the crown of life for us, although it is by no means the end of what God wants to do for us! My prayer is that we would begin to hear and see God work so regularly and clearly in our lives that this verse would be a banner over us. That His saving acts woud be so numerous we would begin to lose count.

These saving acts look like, many times, God speaking to us. Why? Because when He speaks to us and imparts His wisdom and will for any given situation, we are "saved" from wrong thinking, wrong decisions, and wrong actions!

Jot down a way that God has "spoken" to you in the past. If you can't recall a time, list some ways that you think God could speak.

The title of this lesson is the admonition we should heed as we dive into some different ways that God may speak to us. I know all of this has the propensity for abuse, so I will state the foundation on which it will be laid. What He tells us will never, never contradict Scripture. Our Bible is the infallible word (meaning without error), complete, and will stand eternally as God's witness of Himself. (See 1 Peter 1:24-25.) I am not an advocate of people barking like dogs "in the Spirit" because there is no foundation for it in the Scripture. We see people "falling down like dead men" (Revelation 1:17) and being "sore afraid" (Luke 2:9) when God showed up, but I don't see anyone handling poisonous snakes on purpose! So whatever we are "hearing" from God *must* align with the truth of His word, no question. On the other hand, when we see it in His word, we mustn't be afraid of it!

Spiritual discernment is very important. When Jesus was tempted in the wilderness by the devil in Matthew 4, the enemy himself quoted Psalm 91:11-12 to Jesus! Psalm 91:11-12 is truth right? Jesus had the discernment to know that those particular verses did not apply to Him at that time. Sure, He could have "claimed" it over His life, but what did He say? He answered with a Scripture that the Father told Him to apply in that situation, "You shall not put the Lord your God to the test." (Deut. 6:16, NASB)

Please read 1 John 4:1.

Some safety nets we have been given to test the spirits are to compare what we are hearing to other Scriptures, to take what you believe you are hearing to godly authorities, and the confirmation of the Holy Spirit inside of you along with God confirming His Word to you in one or more of the ways listed over the next couple of days.

We are going to look at 10 different ways that God spoke to people in the Bible. This list is not exhaustive, but it is a good start to help us discern Him more clearly as we seek to hear His voice.

The first five are:

1. He speaks through His written Word (the Bible).

2. He speaks through other people.

3. He speaks through circumstances.

4. He may speak through His still, small voice.

5. He speaks through our own conscience.

For the sake of room, we are going to look at one passage for each of these (although there are more).

1. He speaks through His word. Please read Acts 23:1-5.
Paul was convicted of what he said by, I believe, the Holy Spirit bringing to his mind the Word of God. He was referencing Exodus 22:28.

2. He speaks through other people. Please read Acts 9:17.
God used Ananias to tell Saul what His "word" for him was.

3. He speaks through circumstances. Please read Acts 12:3-17.
They were praying fervently and God answered through circumstances, giving them what they prayed for, and they couldn't believe it!

4. He speaks through a still, small voice. Please read 1 Kings 19:11-12.
This is a fairly famous passage on God speaking. This could be a quiet voice in your heart that you know did not come from you. "My sheep hear my voice and I know them and they follow Me." (John 10:27, ESV)

5. Our conscience. Please read Romans 2:14-16.
Sometimes I have heard this called a "check in our spirit." The Holy Spirit works through a believer's conscience to convict or aquit us. He tells us right from wrong, good from best.

Well, five more ways are coming tomorrow! Start looking for Him to speak to you through these ways even today!

How exciting You are Lord! Your attributes never change, but the way You work in our lives is new and ever-changing if we look with spiritual eyes. Open our hearts to understand these deeds of salvation that You are working for us all the time. In Jesus name, amen.

WEEK 2 MEMORY VERSE:

"The voice of the LORD is powerful;
the voice of the LORD is majestic."
Psalm 29.4 (NASB)

WEEK 2
DAY 2

Test the Spirits continued...

Are we ready for the next five? My prayer is that some of those ways that God can speak to us were already familiar to you and it renewed your desire to hear Him more. If none of them were familiar — then how exciting! The eyes of your heart have been enlightened as to how to recognize His voice more clearly.

Here is the foundational truth that this lesson is going to be prefaced with: God (the Trinity) is the same today, yesterday and forever. (Hebrews 13:8 NASB) If the Bible says it to be true about God and the way He works, we can believe that it continues to be true about God and the way He works. The areas that we are going to cover can have the potential to cause some skepticism and rightfully so. The "abuse", as we "conservative" Christians tend to call it, happened from the formation of the Christian church (read 1 & 2 Corinthians) and continues today. Even so, it does not negate that God can speak in these ways today, to whomever He wants, as He sees fit.

Being filled with the same wonder at what God is doing to advance His kingdom here on earth did not end when Peter and Paul died! (See Acts 2:43.) It came from Jesus then and Jesus is very much alive today. Did He not die so that we could experience Him in all His fullness? Colossians 2:9-10a says, "For in Him (that is Jesus) dwelleth all the fullness of the Godhead bodily. And ye are complete in Him..." Let's go back to the Bible, see how God revealed Himself there, and be aware that He can reveal Himself in the same ways today. This is all so that we can know Him better, obey Him, and become more like Christ.

Continuing in our list of ways God spoke in the Scriptures, let's add:

6. He speaks through angels.
7. He speaks through dreams.
8. He speaks through visions.
9. He speaks through trances.
10. He speaks through Jesus.

I found out something interesting the first time this lesson was presented to a group of young women. Most of us at the time were attending churches that would be labeled as "solid", "conservative", and "Bible-teaching." Many of us had never heard a pulpit teach on these subjects in our entire lives. Even so, as I listed them off and began to define them, testimonies began to pop up from all around the room. "I had that happen to me, I just didn't know what to call it!" "I had a dream just the other night, but I didn't know what to make of it until right now." "God has given me a very specific vision about such and such." These were dedicated Christians that love the Lord and His Word and are raising godly families. It was just neat to know that all of us there weren't kooky. That these things still happen today and have the potential to be a powerful catalyst for hearing God and changing lives. So as we look at some Scriptural references remember they are not exhaustive.

He speaks through angels. Please read Acts 10:1-7.
Cornelius was given a word from God through an angel. Can you think of other times that God spoke through angels? List them below.

He speaks through dreams. Please read Matthew 2:12.
The wise men that came to see Jesus and worship Him were warned in a dream not to return to Herod when leaving the country. List any other times you can recall God speaking to someone in a dream.

He speaks through visions. Please read Acts 18:9.
The Lord spoke to Paul in a vision. Also read Genesis 15:1 and record what happened in that verse.

He speaks through trances. Please read Acts 10:10.
Peter falls into a trance and the Lord speaks to him about His plan for the Gentiles.

Read also Acts 22:17. This is Paul falling into a trance when he was praying in the temple.

Before we move on to the next one, let me give you the definitions of a *vision* and a *trance* directly out of the original language.

Vision~ (*machazeh* in Hebrew) apparition, sight
Trance~ (*ekstasis* in Greek) to remove out of its place or state. An ecstasy in which the mind is, for a time, carried out of or beyond itself and lost. When the use of external senses are suspended and God reveals something in a peculiar manner. (Key Word Study Bible, Exec. Ed. Spiros Zodhiates)

These two tend to be the most outlandish sounding of the whole bunch. They sound "New Age" to us, "mystical"....just plain weird really. How about scary? Here is the thing. There is such thing as scary. There are such things as taro cards and bringing up spirits from the dead and manifestations of demons. Those things are Satan's counterfeits and the Bible says that we, as God's children, are to have nothing to do with! Have absolutely nothing to do with horoscopes, palm readings or séances. He wants us only to look to Him for everything. Let us not believe that what God has appointed as ways to reveal Himself to us are to be shied away from just because Satan has tried to mimic it! Horoscopes are a counterfeit to seeking God and His future plans for us. Levitation and meditation and nirvana are just satanic tries to compare with God's visions and God's trances and God's plan for our eternal existance.

My goal in writing this is not for you to seek these things out so that you can say God spoke to you in these ways. Some exalt themselves because God has used a unique way to reveal Himself to them. Hogwash. If the Lord gives you a Scripture from your child as an answer to a heart's cry you have, it is just as noteworthy! My goal is for you to see them in Scripture, seek the God of the Bible with all your heart and not be scared if He chooses to reveal Himself to you in these ways. The exposure to these will give you the faith to believe that it just might be God Himself speaking so that you can obey whatever He tells you through them.

He speaks through Jesus. Read Hebrews 1:1-2.

This sweet, sweet voice of our Good Shepherd is how I came to salvation. O to learn it and obey it! Jesus' voice does not come with condemnation. It does not come without the room for repentance and recovery. His is the sweetest voice we can ever know. He is real and He sits at the right hand of the Father ever listening and responding to His children when they seek Him. Believe He is real. Imagine His face ever present for you to seek but don't stop there. He also has a response for you. You can know Him. You can know His heart. You can know His will and His thoughts towards you and your situation.

Lord, speak to us however You choose. We are open to what Your Word says You will do and we are sorry if our unbelief keeps You from working and moving freely. (Matthew 13:58 NKJV) If we are going to put You in a box, let it be the box of Scripture that says You are an Almighty God and nothing is impossible for You.

WEEK 2 MEMORY VERSE:

"The voice of the LORD is powerful;
the voice of the LORD is majestic."
Psalm 29:4 (NASB)

WEEK 2
DAY 3

A Humble God

*A*nyone have a visitation from an angel last night? A trance? (I am semi-joking.) I do hope there is more of an awareness of His presence in your life. What a glorious, powerful God! Full of wonders and clothed in majesty. The whole earth does His bidding and all things are under His feet.

> Psalm 113:4-6 (NASB)
> "The LORD is high above all nations;
> His glory is above the heavens.
> Who is the like the LORD our God,
> Who is enthroned on high,
> Who *humbles* Himself to behold
> [to see, to inspect, to really understand and examine]
> the things that are in heaven and in the earth?"

If you have done any study on major world religions, you know that this passage is what sets Christianity apart from all else. We have a great God, enthroned on high (but other religions claim to have that), whose glory is above the heavens (other gods have this glory said about them). But which religion has a god who "humbles himself?" None. Some religions call it blasphemy to say that our God stoops down to care about us, to pick us up out of the pit, forgive us and to *talk* with us? A God Who will share His heart with mere humans? One Who desires to have a relationship with *us*? Never. Not one other religion that I know of has these wild but true claims about their god. The extent of how our God humbles Himself doesn't stop there. He also does all of this without ONE righteous deed required of us. Not ONE. Belief in Jesus Christ, God's Son, is all we have to "do."

Did you know the Koran omits the part of God interacting and talking with His creation in their creation story? Yet this is the key and fundamental truth of Christianity. I will say this many times and never tire of it, it is why Jesus agreed to come and die. The purpose of His death and blood was to reconcile us to our Creator and allow us relational access to Him.

If our God is willing to humble Himself to stoop down and communicate with us, let us be humble enough to gratefully hear Him and obey.

No karma, no self-abasement, no good works will get us in this kind of relationship with God. Only Jesus. This God-man, Jesus, humbled Himself to do what He did for us. Please read Philippians 2:5-11 (The Message).

"Think of yourselves the way Christ Jesus thought of himself. He had equal status with God but didn't think so much of himself that he had to cling to the advantages of that status no matter what. Not at all. When the time came, he set aside the privileges of deity and took on the status of a slave, became human! Having become human, he stayed human. It was an incredibly humbling process. He didn't claim special privileges. Instead, he lived a selfless, obedient life and then died a selfless, obedient death—and the worst kind of death at that—a crucifixion. Because of that obedience, God lifted him high and honored him far beyond anyone or anything, ever, so that all created beings in heaven and on earth—even those long ago dead and buried—will bow in worship before this Jesus Christ, and call out in praise that he is the Master of all, to the glorious honor of God the Father."

Did any of that passage speak to you? Write your thoughts below.

He shed His perfect blood, to be put on the perfect altar made without hands, to make us perfect before the Father. What could we do in response to our humble God? What could you do right now? Write it down and then take the time to do what you have written.

When we cry out for God to reveal Himself to us, it is a humbling thing. It means that we don't have it all together. It shows that we need Him.

Bartimaus was not "cool" for yelling out at Jesus (see Mark 10:46-52). David was loathed by his wife for his worship to his God (see 2 Samuel 6:16). The Father that ran out to meet His prodigal son would have been scoffed at by all His neighbors, for to run in that culture was extremely uncouth (see Luke 15:20). After seeing how God has humbled Himself for us, are there any areas of pride that are keeping you from following Jesus's footsteps? Is the Holy Spirit bringing anything specific to mind? Journal it below and then let's repent. Life is too short to let sin linger.

Thank You, Jesus, for humbling Yourself. It is the reason why we are here. Your humility leaves heaven wide open for our taking! May we be humble as You are. May we show others what recipients of such grace and love should truly look like. For Your fame and glory and in Jesus's name, Amen.

Week 2 Memory Verse:

"The voice of the LORD is powerful;
the voice of the LORD is majestic."
Psalm 29:4 (NASB)

WEEK 2
DAY 4

"A God Who Humbles"

I think it is amazing to have any genre of Christian music available to listen to on YouTube. One particular evening I started a song and put my face towards the floor to sing it to Him (this is good for me to do in the privacy of my own home; I think I am painful to the people that stand next to me at church). Just as I started singing, the Lord began to speak to my heart.

"Stay low, My child. Stay low. But know that it is my heart to lift you up. Humility comes before honor. You stay low; I will do the lifting of your head. Always take the seat at the end of the table and let Me be the One to move you as I will. Stay humble under My mighty hand, I will lift you up."

What moved me the most is when He said, "It is My heart to lift you up."

I felt like the Savior, at whose feet I was sitting, was reaching down and lifting my face up out of the floor. There is a verse that says God will not share His glory with another, nor would we be happy if we took any of God's glory for ourselves. We are the happiest when God is most glorified. And we are happiest when He is glorified through us. When we are a vessel that experiences then displays the God of glory. Throwing ourselves at His feet is completely necessary and appropriate in His presence. Yet also know that He is the glory and the lifter of our heads. We cannot "kiss the Son" (Psalm 2:12) unless our faces are lifted and close to His. We cannot hear His whispers if we are not close to Him. In Christ, we are no longer enemies of God. We are no longer enemies, unable to come into His presence because, in Christ, we are holy and have full access to His throne.

We are going to look at some different ways that we can be humbled after hearing God speak to us. The first is being humbled in the sense of being tempted to feel "humiliated" because of other people's responses to what we have heard. Stick with me, it sounds complicated but it's not.

Please read Genesis 37:5-10. What was God's "word" to Joseph?

What was the reaction of the people around him?

Do you think that could have caused Joseph some humiliation? The people around him obviously didn't think too highly of what he had been told. In fact, it was the catalyst they used to formulate their heartless plan to get rid of him once and for all. (Some of this sounds like what happened to Jesus does it not?) Later on, we are going to tackle the subject of what to do when circumstances don't seem to match up with the given "word" for a time, but for now, we are just focusing on how to avoid the "pit of humiliation." This is the pit that would lead us to think we would rather not hear from God anymore, when our responses from others are less than encouraging.

What are some ways that we can respond when others are a "wet blanket" on our fire to seek the Lord and hear from Him?

It is good to have a foreknowledge of these "wet blankets" and how we would handle them. In order to keep them from doing what Satan intends for them to do. He intends for them to put out your fire. If we are on the lookout for them, we can stand stronger through them. I am not advocating that if a Godly person questions what you've heard with a heart of accountability, that you should consider them a tool of the enemy. There is a difference between someone, in disbelief and doubt, trying to snidely push you in the pit of humiliation (like Joseph's brothers), and another who just wants to make sure that you are hearing correctly. If we have really heard from God, then there should be no fear when a challenge against that "word" comes up.

The much more pleasant way for us to be humbled is when the Lord gives us a "word" that we can utterly rejoice in! Being a thankful and joyful recipient of a "word" from the Lord is humbling. You recognize that you did not speak it, nor can you cause it to happen. Perhaps it is a word of encouragement just when you need it. Maybe it's a promise of His supernatural presence in a hard situation. Or an exciting word for someone else that the Lord gives you the pleasure of passing on to him or her. These humble us also because, "It is beyond all contradiction that it is the lesser person who is blessed by the greater one." (Hebrews 7:7 AMP)

Please read Luke 1: 27-32, 46-55.

This is a great example of being humbled by a "word" we can rejoice in! (Note: Did you know that the Greek word for "rejoice" in verse 47 means to "skip and jump around with joy?" When God tells us awesome things, it is completely appropriate (and Biblical) to jump around a little bit...or a lot. God recently fulfilled a "word" to our family that we had waited 7 years for and we grabbed up our kids and just danced (it looked more like ring-around-the-rosy) in the living room! Rejoice! The Bible says to make His praise *glorious*!

Thirdly, humility comes from opening our hearts to hear rebuke. Rebuke is also something that will keep our noses to the ground (if we are sincerely listening with a heart to obey). We need to learn to love rebuke (oh, this is so painful to write). Well, not the rebuke itself, but the fruit of righteousness rebuke and repentance can grow when we let God have His way. Our hearts need to be *trained* to respond with thankfulness because He disciplines those He loves. Being humbled by a rebuke from the Lord, or someone else (ouch!) is a beautiful, gracious U-turn sign right in the middle of our highway to destruction. There are two ways to respond to this: stiffen our necks or receive and repent. Here is some encouragement to avoid the former and gravitate towards the latter.

Please read Proverbs 25:12. What does it liken a rebuke to?

Please read also Proverbs 29:1. What happened in this verse?

Has there been a time recently where you have been the recipient of a rebuke? How did you respond?

What were the results of how you responded?

Hearing a rebuke from the Lord is for our good. He never intends to shove our faces in the dirt or keep us under some condemning chain. Any and all rebuke is to be coupled with a humble heart that returns back to the One who loves us with an everlasting love.

Let us remain with our faces to the floor and our ears open to hear. He will be the glory and lifter of our heads.

Oh thank You, Lord, for putting us in our proper place. For there is where we experience Your blessing rather than Your mighty hand of discipline. May we stay low so we can rejoice when Your gentle hands lift us up. It is when we stop and humble ourselves that we can hear You more clearly, for we miss You when we barrel along through our life in the pride of self-sufficiency. Abiding in the Vine is where we want to be so we can partake of all You have for us. (John 15: 7-11) We love You! Amen.

WEEK 2 MEMORY VERSE:

"The voice of the LORD is powerful;

the voice of the LORD is majestic."

Psalm 29:4 (NASB)

WEEK 2
DAY 5

"Humbling Ourselves Through Fasting"

You know, since we are supposed to put oil on our heads and wash our faces, there may be a lot of people fasting that I don't know about. Even so, I get a sense that it is an unused element in our tackle box of ways that we seek God. Fasting is a powerful, powerful discipline to engage in, especially in regards to experiencing His presence and hearing His voice.

First, let's define what fasting is. It is abstaining from some foods, all foods, or food and water to seek God. Sometimes it is coupled with repentance (Nehemiah 9:1-3), sometimes with seeking an answer to a prayer request (2 Samuel 12:22-24), but it is always coupled with prayer and/or worship. Fasting in and of itself has some benefits for the body, but without prayer it is just a gesture of self-abasement that will get us nowhere spiritually. God wants us to rend our *hearts*, not our empty sacraments. This is a lengthy passage, but crucial in our understanding of the heart God desires behind our religious alms.

Please read Isaiah 58. Record any of the verse numbers or key phrases below that seemed to jump out at you.

If our relationships with others are not right (and it is in our power to reconcile), fasting won't do us a lick of good in regards to hearing from/experiencing God. Malachi tells us that a husband's prayers are null and void when he is treating his wife with contempt (Malachi 2:13-16), so we can rest assured that humbling ourselves with fasting does not move His heart if we have unresolved issues with others. If we are striking with wicked fists (saying hateful, mean things to each other) all the while claiming that we "desire to know His ways and commands" (Isaiah 58:1-2), we may as well just go to Chick-fil-A (and I really am sorry if you live in an area like I do that doesn't have one). But if we are living at peace and loving everyone (as much as it is in our power to do so), fasting will benefit us greatly. Again, fasting is sometimes coupled with repentance, so if there is a strained relationship that we want healing for, fasting *is* appropriate in that case!

As far as abstaining from things other than food as a "fast," I believe that God is graciously accepting of our offerings. Nevertheless, there is a difference between giving up that which we *need* (food and water) and that which is not necessary for life (ie. computer, candycrush, or chess). There is just something about having a gnawing hunger for necessary sustenance, and instead turning to God to be filled. I understand health issues that keep some people from giving up food altogether (this is where a Daniel or juice fast may be appropriate), and that is fine. However, if that is not the case, then we will continue on with regards to the giving up of food.

Here are some additional Scriptures to look up in regards to fasting. Be encouraged by them as we join some dynamic followers of Christ in humbling ourselves with fasting to hear His voice more clearly.

Esther 4:12-15
Nehemiah 1-2:8
Daniel 9:3,20-23
Luke 2:33-38
Acts 13:2-3

Journal any prayers/thoughts about fasting that you have at the moment. Be honest with the Lord as to where you are and what you are thinking.

Now comes the challenge. Would you commit, with at least one other person, to fasting one meal a week for the duration of this study? Breakfast tends to be the best for me because I can get up early and seek the Lord without distraction (usually). If your kids are in school, or if you have a lunch break that you could go to your car and seek the Lord, lunch might be easier for you. If you have ever fasted, then you already know what I am about to say. But for those who have not ever fasted take comfort and encouragement in this: there has not been a time where fasting has not resulted in my experiencing the presence of God and/or answered prayer. During my times of fasting, I constantly reiterate to the Lord my reason for doing it: that I am serious about seeking Him. I just walk around when I am hungry telling Him that. Fasting is one way to outwardly show how dedicated you are to seeing Him move, seeking His face, or ministering to Him. My personal recommendation is to choose a day and stick to the same one each week. Then your mind can be forewarning your body, which can make it easier. If you would commit to that, would you pray and ask God what day and meal He would like for you to fast and write it below? (Be open! He may tell you to do something different, this is just a suggestion.)

In closing, I appreciate Bill Bright's take on the teaching of fasting found in the Sermon on the Mount (Matthew 5-7). He does not think that fasting has to be done in complete secrecy, only with the proper motives. Wouldn't it be easier if we knew we were all doing this together? Partner up with someone! How much more power and accountability would there be? One of the more lengthy fasts I have ever done, I did with a friend. It helped tremendously to talk about our grumpiness and hunger, but also to sow together in prayer and just walk through it with each other. I remember dreaming about food and waking up thinking I had eaten and broken my word to the

Lord! I had a certain number of requests I was seeking Him about and I was fasting one day per request. Wouldn't you know that I *didn't hear a thing* until the final hours on the last day and I got an answer for every single one! Well, there is a lot of information on the internet about fasting (Bill Bright's being very good and concise), but we know enough to get started.

My prayer for this area of discipline is that we will see God work so mightily through it that there would be a hunger stirred in us to practice it regularly. (No pun intended.)

Lord, I just pray over us that as we seek to hear You through fasting, that You would come in all Your fullness to us. You are what we want, Your presence is better than life. In Jesus' name, amen.

WEEK 2 MEMORY VERSE:

"The voice of the LORD is powerful;
the voice of the LORD is majestic."
Psalm 29:4 (NASB)

WEEK 3
DAY 1

"How Long Must I Wait? (Do not lose heart.)"

I am sure you will be excited to hear this: God has ordained waiting to take up a majority of our lives. We wait 9 months for our baby, we wait in traffic for the green light, and we wait in line at the store...Why does this honor Him? Why would He put this in our existence to have to be dealt with day after day? I believe how we handle waiting on God is a sure sign of our heart's condition. Notice our right perspective...waiting *on God*. We are not waiting for our circumstances to change, we are waiting *on God* to change them or change us...see the difference?

Back on day three of week one, I had shared about John being unemployed. The job that the Lord opened up for him was so far from where we were living that he had to commute home only on the weekends. I was a stay at home mom of a newborn and two other pre-school aged children at the time. John only came home to us late Friday nights and would turn around to go back Sunday afternoons. This schedule had been going on for some time and our emotions were running thin. (I think if he was in the military and we expected for us to be apart it would have been different, but as it was, we were struggling.) We were waiting on the Lord to provide housing for us so we could move closer to John's job. I was getting frustrated. (*Really*? After all God had just done to provide him a job?) Yep. I remember taking it to the Lord Who had something to say to me. It went something like this, "Jana, if you have a bad attitude about this, it shows that it is an idol in your life and you aren't *really* holding it with an open hand." Wow.

I was crossing the line of, "You honor Me with your lips yet your heart is far from Me." (Matthew 15:8) To think that I would exchange the Sovereign God of the universe His rightful place in my heart, for a *house* is crazy when you stop and think about it. How we handle waiting on God can be a sign that we are placing "things" or "circumstances" in front of Him who has every right to do whatever He pleases with it all.

Take a look at how long these people had to wait for the "word" the Lord gave them to come to pass. Jot down what you find:

Abraham had to wait for the promise of Issac? (Genesis 12:4 and 21:5)

Jacob had to wait for Rachel to become his wife? (Genesis 29:19-20 and 29:27)

Israel had to wait to be redeemed from the oppression of Egypt? (Genesis 15:13)

David had to wait from the time he was anointed to be king, until he actually took the throne (running for his life from Saul the entire time)?
(1 Samuel 16:1-13, 2 Samuel 5:4-5)

The disciples had to wait for the promise of the Holy Spirit? (Leviticus 23:16) (Time from the Passover to Pentecost.)

We have had to wait for the second coming of our Lord so far (approximately)?

Waiting is in God's sovereign, mysterious purpose for us. Expect to have to wait for things. It is not easy, but the Bible gives us direction on how to honor God and even encourage others through our waiting on Him.

Please read Psalm 40:1. What characteristic did David exemplify during his time of "waiting on the Lord?"

The original Hebrew word for "patient" here also implies that David's waiting was done with a confident expectation.

Why does it honor God when we wait in that way for Him? Write some thoughts below.

More than that, we are waiting for Jesus to come and make all this mess right.

Hebrews 9:28 (AMP)

"Even so it is that Christ, having been offered to take upon Himself and bear as a burden the sins of many and once for all, will appear a second time, not to carry any burden of sin nor to deal with sin, but to bring to full salvation those who are [eagerly, constantly, and patiently] waiting for and expecting Him."

Again, the very word for "wait" in the Hebrew (and Greek) denotes a hopeful expectation. There is a full assurance that one will receive what they are waiting for. It is said of Abraham in Romans 4 that during his time of waiting he, "did not waver in unbelief, but grew strong in faith, giving glory to God, and being fully assured that what God had promised, He was able to perform."

When God gives us a word for our circumstances, our lives, or for/about someone else, let us have the same faith as Abraham that God will do it. I don't know how long you are going to have to hold on, but you are greatly loved by God and you will receive what He has promised. (Sometimes I feel like I have to remind Him that I am only going to live 80 years at the most though!)

Is there anything you are currently "waiting" on God for?

How is your current attitude towards your waiting?

What, from this lesson, is the Lord saying to you in regards to that which you are waiting on Him for?

You, O God, are faithful to fulfill any and every word You speak. You are faithful when we are faithless. May our attitudes during our times of waiting on You be worthy of Who You are. You are trying to work out an amazingly glorious eternity for us and we are sorry for the times we grumble while we wait for that to be manifested. With a new fervor we put our desires and our futures in Your capable hands. We are hopeful for the ways You are going to work in our lives! Bless You, Lord Jesus. It is in Your name we pray, amen.

Week 3 Memory Verse:

"I waited patiently for the LORD, and He turned to me and heard my cry for help." Psalm 40:1 (HCSB)

WEEK 3
DAY 2

"Working Through the Wait"

Since waiting can be one of the hardest, yet richest times that we go through in our walk with the Lord, we are going to sit here a little longer. I hope the lesson yesterday showed that waiting is ordained to be a regular part of a saint's life. God may even choose to use many years of waiting to fulfill His purposes. I understand if that can seem a bit overwhelming and even a bit discouraging. The part that we don't want to miss is the stuff that happens in the middle.

You might have heard it said that, "the journey is just as important as the destination." John and I had to wait a long time (respectively) for God to bring us together. We were not married until he was 33 and I was 27. But thank you God for his years of singleness! He learned how to cook and do laundry and clean (well, kind of). I can remember at times feeling like it was really hard to wait on God for my mate. At other times it was easier. I am currently waiting on God for two important things in my own life at this time. Of course, like most things we wait on, when we finally get them, the time we waited seems like a mere breath. I know what it's like for a week to feel like a month and a month to feel like a year.

Today's purpose is two fold: to find out what we should do during our wait and what we can expect from God in our seasons of waiting.

You know, some things that we wait on are not that big of a deal. We can move on with life around us and just pull it out to pray about every once in a while…then there are the things that seem larger than life and we can't spend a minute without it coming back into our thoughts. Those things are the hardest to keep in perspective and under God's sovereign authority and love. They are the things that really test our trust in Him, that really reveal our hearts, as we talked about yesterday. So what do we do to walk through the waiting with victory and confidence? Enjoy the lyrics to this Spirit-ordained song:

By: John Waller

I'm waiting
I'm waiting on You, Lord
And I am hopeful

I'm waiting on You, Lord
Though it is painful
But patiently, I will wait

I will move ahead, bold and confident
Taking every step in obedience
While I'm waiting
I will serve You
While I'm waiting
I will worship
While I'm waiting
I will not faint
I'll be running the race
Even while I wait

I'm waiting
I'm waiting on You, Lord
And I am peaceful
I'm waiting on You, Lord
Though it's not easy
But faithfully, I will wait

He must have read Psalm 40:1. This song has a great list of things that we are to do while we wait on the Lord. He speaks of being hopeful, confident, peaceful...what an honoring way to wait on the Lord. Our worship needs to continue during our times of waiting, our service needs to continue and we need to continue to walk in step with the Spirit for He has plans for every day. Now those are things we can actively do on our part while we wait. What is God's part? What can we (because we see it in Scripture) expect from God while we are putting forth all this effort to wait patiently?

This is a very important part of hearing from God. Because waiting takes up a lot of our lives and some things can be very difficult to wait on, I believe firmly that we need the Holy Spirit to give us something specific and tangible from the Lord to somehow see us through those times. Some promises always apply to us such as, "I will never leave you or forsake you" (Hebrews 13:5). "All things work together for good for those who love God and are called according to His purpose" (Romans 8:28). These are awesome and can be claimed at all times as God's children, but let me give you an example of what I mean about needing some kind of word from God for a specific situation.

There was a difficult season I was in recently, and a friend told me, "You know, God is going to do whatever He wants," so basically, "don't worry about it." Well, that didn't work for me. I had a bonafide fear that I needed a "word" for. I didn't care *what* God said about it, as long as He said *something* I could fix my mind on to battle the thoughts the enemy was throwing at me. To my comfort and sanity, He gave me a "word" to stand on. It wasn't even a word that told me my fear wouldn't ever come to pass. It was just a word that redeemed my soul and let me know that He was in control. I continue to pull it out every so often when those old feelings creep in, but the battle doesn't have to last long. Resist the devil and he will flee from you. Having a direct, specific "word" from the Lord is one of the most powerful weapons against his schemes we have! So when you get that "(s)word", swing it Sister!

Lets look at the example of Abraham. God had spoken His promise to Abram, first recorded, in Genesis 12. He promised that He would make of him (who had no children) a great nation and give him possession of the land of Israel. He also told Abram to leave his family and just start walking. In faith, Abram packed up his entire family and left the next morning. The years passed. I am sure it was tempting for Abram to wonder about the truth of these promises, but the Bible tells us that he held fast to his faith without wavering. How did he do that? I want to suggest because God continued to encourage him by repeating His promise to him during the course of his waiting. In fact, here are all the times that God re-confirmed His promise to Abraham while he waited.

Genesis 13:14-17

Genesis 15

Genesis 17

Genesis 18:1-15

As with Abraham, the waiting is a lot easier when you continue to hear the Lord confirming that He remembers you and what He has said. So we can look for this from the Lord. He knows that we are but dust. These reminders keep our minds stayed on Him, keeps our hope confident, keeps us from being faint. So we can continue to walk in whatever God has for us each day, confidently knowing that Genesis 21:1 will happen in our lives too.

"THE LORD took note of Sarah *as He had said, and the Lord did for Sarah as He had promised.*" (NASB, emphasis added)

Yay! The laughter of unbelief was turned into the laughter of unspeakable joy! The labor of waiting was over and the promise was birthed. And Abraham is noted as being one of the most faith-filled men in scripture. He is called the "Father" of many nations because he heard God speak His promises and he believed them even to his death.

So our part is to listen for God to speak and believe Him when He does! Then as we wait for Him to work out that particular thing, we hold fast in faith, patient and unwavering for He is faithful.

O Lord, if there is anyone waiting on you for something that is seeming to take a long time, would You visit them again, through this lesson, and continue to confirm that You remember them. Confirm that You are aware of exactly where they are at and that You are still working out Your perfect plan. O weary one, hold fast! Your Redeemer is called Faithful and True! In Jesus' name, amen.

Week 3 Memory Verse:

"I waited patiently for the LORD, and He turned to me and heard my cry for help." Psalm 40:1 (HCSB)

WEEK 3
DAY 3

"It All Comes Down to FAITH"

In light of eternity, our stay here is short and our fleeting years of waiting are even shorter (even when they don't seem so fleeting). During these waiting periods we need encouragement because we are in "time" and have known nothing else. Our clocks continue to tick day after day and never stop, but God is in a realm that is not bound by time. Even so, God has required something of us on this side of heaven that we cannot get around...faith. To believe what we cannot see and to believe we will see it one day. Remember, this faithful waiting is not all for naught!

Would you wait?
In the faith a little longer
Raise your head
He's coming soon

Would you pray?
Watch for just another hour
For His word to you
Will come true

Would you stay?
In the pain a few more years
For an eternity
Of bliss

Oh we will be so glad we stayed
We will be so glad we stayed
In the faith

A hundred times over we will! When we finally stand face to face with Jesus wouldn't we rather fall at His feet proclaiming, "I did my best Lord! I did everything You told me to do!" We will be so glad we trusted Him. We will be so glad we held fast to Him. There is one word that causes us to do that with gusto: FAITH.

Define faith in your own words.

This is a silly little acronym the Lord gave me. (Well, if I believe it was Him, maybe I shouldn't call it silly.)

F~ully
A~ssured
I~n [the]
T~ruth [you've]
H~eard

What does a faith-filled person look like? What attributes would you use to describe them?

When was there a time in your life that you can remember really, fully, trusting God to do what He promised? How did you feel? Briefly describe it below.

When was there a time in your life when you went through something and didn't fully trust God? How did you feel? Briefly describe it below.

The most popular verses about faith are found in Hebrews 11. It is often called the "Hall of Faith" of believers who walked this road before us. Let's look at it with fresh eyes today. Starting with verse 1, define below what the Bible says Faith is.

This may take a few minutes, but skim through Hebrews 11 and make a list of things that others did "by faith" with the verse reference next to it. I will give two examples below.

By faith Abel offered a better sacrifice and was called righteous. vs. 4
By faith, Abel still speaks though he is dead. vs. 4

Did any of the things you read apply to something that you are going through today? Do you need encouragement that God can "raise something from the dead" in your life? Do you need to know that by faith, you can deny the passing pleasures of sin to gain Christ? Pick the one that applies to your life and ask/believe God for it. Be fully assured that your steadfast faith in our Almighty God is witnessed by Him and will be commended by Him in the presence of all of heaven one day!

Tell Him you believe Him today. Spend some time really declaring how faithful He is and how His promises will never fail. If we do this, our souls will start responding with that same confidence.

Week 3 Memory Verse:

"I waited patiently for the LORD, and He turned to me and heard my cry for help." (HCSB)

WEEK 3
DAY 4
"Watch Out That Your Faith Doesn't Fail"

So what would make us (we who are seeking His face, hearing His heart, and trying to live in faith) unfruitful in our lives? Let's bring to the light three things that we need to watch for when seeking to hear from God with the intent to obey. They come from Matthew 13:3-9. Please read those verses and list the 3 things that caused the "seed" to be *un*fruitful.

1.

2.

3.

Now let's read Matthew 13:18-23 and define what each of those 3 things acually represent.

1.

2.

3.

Jesus is speaking about hearing the "logos" (or word) of the Kingdom of God. Logos (in a simplified definition) means "intelligent, understandable speech." This is so cool: Jesus is called *ho Logos* in John 1 meaning first, immaterial intelligence and secondly, the expression of that intelligence in speech that humans could understand. (Key Word Greek and Hebrew Study Bible, pg. 1832) God came down and spoke of His salvation, His kingdom, and His eternal plans for the universe *in a language that we, as humans, have the ability to understand.* In contrast, John 8:43 tells us that Jesus was speaking to His people (the Jews) and He told them they were not able to understand His logos. Why? In the Greek language because they really *did not want* to hear the truth and obey it. Which leads us to a very important point. The "soil" of our hearts is a huge factor in regards to fruitfulness.

God's Word will never return void and will always accomplish the purpose God had for it, but the preparation of the soil is, in some mysterious way, *our* responsibility. Jeremiah 4:3 and Hosea 10:12 both talk about the people of God "breaking up their fallow ground."

Good soil takes some time to build up. Rocks have to be dug out, weeds must be pulled. Rocks and weeds are pictures of sin and selfishness in our lives. We have to allow the Holy Spirit access to every part of our souls to get these things out. They come out with confession and repentance. I want to suggest that a soft, open heart (with every known thing repented of), humility and love towards others and God, are sure signs that the soil of your heart is able to receive the seed of the Word and have it bear fruit in your life. This heart of good soil looks at the Word of God with a decision *already made* to obey what it says. Oh, but we mustn't forget the Holy Spirit in this process! We can read the Bible all day long and miss what Jesus is personally saying to us through it. For example, when I was praying just this morning, the Lord brought to my mind the verse that says, "...they will know you are Christians by your love for one another." (John 13:35) I was repenting of a sharp, unkind comment I had made to one of my family members. Wouldn't you know that same verse was the Bible Gateway verse of the day that morning?! That was reading the Word with the Holy Spirit personally applying it to me! The quality of the soil of my heart will show in how I take that verse and obey it!

Which of the three things listed in Matthew, do you think personally threatens your faith-filled fruitfulness the most? Journal your thoughts below.

What do you think it looks like when the word of God produces fruit 100, 60, and 30 fold?

Think about your main threat against your fruitfulness that you wrote about earlier. What are some ways you can combat it?

Share what God has shown you with others! You may have some insight that could tremendously help someone else bear more fruit. Others can, in turn, help you avoid the pitfalls these scriptures talk about.

O Lord, we want to bear fruit—100 fold!! As we prepare our hearts to hear You through Your word with repentance, humility, and determination to obey whatever You say, would You work such a harvest in our lives?! We want reward, not regret, when we see You face to face. In Jesus's name. Amen.

WEEK 3 MEMORY VERSE:

"I waited patiently for the LORD, and He turned to me and heard my cry for help." Psalm 40:1 (HCSB)

WEEK 3
DAY 5

Yesterday's lesson ended with encouragement to tell someone else what God has been showing you. God has put us in this thing He calls a "family" for a reason. His plan is that we should need each other on this side of heaven. Would you start off today by reading Proverbs 18:1? What does it tell us about "sound wisdom"?

The NASB translation says that when we separate ourselves from others, seeking our own desires, we quarrel against *all* sound wisdom. Wow. The Body of Christ is indispensable to us. God knows that if we were left to our own devices and desires, we would end up in less than desirable places! Others can keep us on track, keep our heads "out of the clouds," and help keep our faith strong. Hebrews 4:13 tells us of the great need we have for each other's encouragement.

"But encourage one another day after day, as long as it is still called 'Today,' lest any one of you be hardened by the deceitfulness of sin." (NASB)

Do you have at least one other trusted Christian friend that you can spill your guts to, share your joys with, and truly fellowship with? If so, name them below.

I do not believe that we can be best friends with everyone. We only have so much time in a day to nurture relationships. We can agape (unconditional, God-love) all people, but phileo (brotherly) and storge (family/affectionate) loves are, I believe, really meant for only a handful of people in our lives. We mentioned this earlier in the study, but be watchful about who your phileo and storge friends are. Choose people that spur you on in Christ and don't be afraid to back away from those that don't. It is not by accident that we fulfill Hebrews 4:13. We must build those types of relationships *on purpose*. What does this have to do with hearing from God and obeying Him, you ask? A lot.

1. You cannot and others cannot help you live to your fullest potential in Christ if you are not actively connected to the Body of Christ. This is your responsibility. Your friend cannot

help you obey what the Lord is telling you if you do not share what the Lord is telling you to do and ask for that accountability.

2. Other people can help us discern whether or not we are really hearing the Lord. Our family just watched God do a very fast and amazing turn around in another family. Some people questioned (rightfully so) and we were able to help confirm that what was going on was really of God because of the relationship we had with them. If godly people in your life are questioning, take it to the Lord again and get clarity. Other people can keep us from making unnecessary mistakes or spur us to continue on the right path.

3. Your and my obedience to the Lord affects the entire Body of Christ across the world. Your prayer or lack of prayer is impacting someone somewhere. My actually sitting down to write this out of obedience to the Lord is or has affected someone that might not have been otherwise. Don't underestimate the power that your listening to the Holy Spirit and obeying brings to the Body of Christ as a whole. Will God's sovereign purpose prevail if you and I are not doing what we are supposed to be doing? Yes. Even so, God has set it up that we are able to join Him in His work and it is He that has given us that priviledge.

Please read 1 Corinthians 12:14, 25-26. Did any part of these verses stick out to you, or cause you to see the Body of Christ in a different light? Explain below.

Our relationship with God is not fully alive apart from having relationship with others. That is one mistake of people who isolate themselves "for God." To take ourselves "out of this world" in order to properly live for God is not Biblical.

Again, here are some reasons we need others as we seek to hear God and obey whatever He tells us. God wants to use other people to show us Himself in new ways and to help support us through this life. Some things we hear from God will need to be bounced off another believer for confirmation. Others can spur us on to obey what He has told us when we feel like giving up. There is much power in group prayer, group worship, and group ministry. We need each other and we need to be for each other what the Word tells us to be. We need to be compassionate and gracious, kindhearted and forgiving. Jesus said that the whole world would know that we were Christians by the love we have for one another.

Pray and ask God to begin to show you who and how you need to be fellowshiping and ministering with. Follow through immediately with whatever He tells you to do. It may be to call someone and encourage them to keep going! It may be to call someone *for* encouragement to keep going! If you do not currently have a friend like this, pray for the Lord to bring someone that you can have a Christ-centered friendship with.

Help us to lay aside petty arguments and dissensions so that we can shine like stars in the universe in relationship to You and each other. Show us ways to encourage our closest friends and those in the Body of Christ daily so we can fulfill Your word in Hebrews 4:13. Give us understanding of this reality that we are "one" with those who know You! In Jesus's name, amen.

Week 3 Memory Verse:

"I waited patiently for the LORD, and He turned to me and heard my cry for help." Psalm 40:1 (HCSB)

WEEK 4
DAY 1

"God's Requirement for Discipleship"

One of the most mysterious things about God in my opinion, is the unknowable chasm between God's sovereignty and man's responsibility. I don't get it. I just know it's there. God has a part and we have a part. I cannot do His part and He will not do my part. Just hearing from Him is not enough...we have a responsibility to do something with it–to obey what we hear. This is a requirement of God to prove that we are truly His disciples.

James 1:25 says, "But one who looks intently at the perfect law, the law of liberty, and abides by it, not having become a forgetful hearer but an effectual doer, this man will be blessed in what he does." (NASB)

Obeying the Word of God (the Bible) and obeying what the Spirit leads you to do as you walk with Him moment by moment, is our part. His part is to reveal Himself through His word (or any of the other ways we talked about in week two) to us. His part is to aid us and strengthen us to complete the tasks He gives and to keep us sealed until the day our salvation is made sight. He will always be faithful. You will never lack what you need to obey God. He has made sure of that by giving us the Holy Spirit who lives inside of us...our part is to *surrender.*

No matter where you or I find ourselves in life, "small" sins, "large" sins, apathy towards God or worse, there is forgiveness and a new chance to start over. The Bible says that repentance brings refreshment to our souls, so we turn again to the Lover of our souls and believe His love stands ready to receive us. Take some time and offer the Lord a sacrifice of repentance if there is an area of your life that you need to surrender completely to Him. If you cannot think of one practice hearing from God and ask Him to reveal anything that may be hidden in your soul. Jot your thoughts/prayers below.

Do we think that complete surrender to the Lord is going to involve us living in a hut miles from civilization without the ability to shave our legs for the rest of our lives, hating every moment of it? Well, God may call you to a hut, but if your heart is fully surrendered **to God**, *not just the "call,"* I promise you will be fulfilled beyond your every dream and wish.

Why?

Because you will have ***God***.

Repentance and surrender brings His life into our situation. Death comes when we move forward in our flesh, or in our own stubborn self-will in any given situation.

Describe a time that you chose the way of death, rather than listening to the Lord and obeying?

From the beginning, God set up some requirements for discipleship if we were to choose to believe in His Son. Read the following verses and list those "requirements" that you find in them.

Luke 14:25-27

Mark 8:34-38

What does Luke 9:26 say about our attitude towards believing in and following God's Word?

Jesus wasn't too "seeker friendly" when it came to His requirement for discipleship, it seems. In some cases, it even sounds as though He is even trying to talk people out of following Him.

Did you receive Christ knowing that He required such commitment and surrender from you? Journal your thoughts below.

In what ways have your thoughts towards discipleship changed since the time where you first heard of/received Christ?

This lesson is not at all meant to condemn us, it is meant to sober us up. Are we really ready to follow what He tells us, or are we just excited that the Lord is going to speak? Our choice to follow Jesus is a serious thing and requires much of us...actually...*all* of us. We are told to "work out our salvation with fear and trembling." (Philippians 2:12 NASB) This salvation is a precious gift. It is not given lightly and not to be taken lightly. Let's "raise the bar" on how we view it and our lives in light of it. This is where the second part of the word "azan" comes in. Not just hearing what He has to say, but already surrendered to obeying what He says, because of what He has done for us. It...He, is and will be found worthy of our complete surrender.

Father, we surrender. You love us–we trust You. Tell us whatever Your will is and we will follow You. To the ends of the earth or to the grave, You deserve our obedience because of what You have done for us. How silly to waste our lives by doing our own will rather than Yours. Lead us on, cross and all. For Your name Jesus, amen.

WEEK 4 MEMORY VERSE:

"And He was saying to them all, 'If anyone wants to come with Me, he must deny himself, and take up his cross daily and follow Me'." Luke 9:23 (HCSB)

WEEK 4
DAY 2

Surrender vs. Idolatry

As the Lord brought the title of this lesson to mind, I thought, "Is surrender really the opposite of idolatry?"

Please read 1 Samuel 15:23. What does it define "idolatry" as?

If surrender is everything we talked about yesterday–being completely God's and giving up the rights to our own life–it *is* the opposite of idolatry. Idolatry is sometimes viewed as external "things" that we put before God, but of all those "things", stubbornness and self-will is at the heart of them. The dictionary defines stubbornness as: "obstinate, fixed or set in purpose or opinion." Namely ours rather than God's. The background to the verse in 1 Samuel was when Saul did not completely obey the Word of the Lord by *utterly* destroying the Amalekites. He left the best of the flocks and spared the king also. But that was not what God had commanded Saul to do. How scary to know that partial surrender is not surrender in God's eyes. Partial surrender cost Saul his kingship. (See 1 Samuel 15:26.) God is seeking people that will follow Him wholeheartedly and will obey Him completely.

Why do you think partial surrender/obedience is considered idolatry to God?

What are some reasons that keep us from obeying God fully?

You might have written "fear" somewhere in that list. Saul's partial obedience was out of "fear" of the people if you read the whole passage in 1 Samuel. Matthew 25 speaks of three servants that were each given a different amount of money to steward and grow while their Master was away. Two of the three servants doubled their money by being wise with it and even taking some risks with it. The third servant went and hid the bag of money in the ground and did nothing with it to try to multiply it. The Master came back, rewarded the other two servants with great reward, and turned to this third servant who said, "Master...I was afraid and went away and hid your talent in the ground. See, you have what is yours." What we need to notice (and this is scary) is that the servant said he was what? Afraid. But if we look at verse 26, the Master reveals what is at the root of fear. He did not answer compassionately and pat the guy's head telling him He understood... he called him two things: wicked and lazy. *Wicked and lazy?* Fear of man proves to be a snare Proverbs tells us. Paul said that if he were to fear man and not God, he would not be a servant of God. I believe that fear is probably the number one reason we choose to either partially obey God or not obey Him at all. It is eye-opening to think that God sees this as being wicked and lazy. Oh, but God is such a gracious God! Don't think that if something really, really scares you, that He will not comfort you as He leads you to do it. He comforted Joshua over and over with the words, "Be strong and courageous, do not be afraid for the Lord your God is with you wherever you go!" But we cannot let the fear lead us to the unbelief that God will not do His part. That is where the wickedness comes in. God also knew that the servant was partially using that as an excuse because he was lazy. The servant didn't want to put forth the effort needed to complete the task of stewardship that was given him. Now, with that parable in mind, is there anything that comes to your mind that you have failed to obey God fully on and how does it make you feel knowing that wickedness and laziness could be at the root of it? Journal your thoughts below.

Is there anything in your life currently that you are "obstinately fixed or set in your own opinion" about? If so, write it below. Repent and take time in prayer to give the Lord complete control over it.

The dictionary definition for surrender is: "to yield to the possession or power of another." It goes hand in hand with submission. Since we have used Saul as an example of someone who did not completely surrender, let's look at his successor.

Please read Acts 13:22. What did God say of David in these verses?

The Amplified Bible says in verse 22 that David was chosen because he would "carry out My (God's) program *fully*." Wouldn't you love to have had that said of you generations after you had lived? That your heart was one that carried out His plans to the *fullest*? David was just a man, but he was a man who completely surrendered to the will of God. Oh, he made his mistakes and suffered their consequences...but this testimony of him is still true and from David's seed was the Messiah born to save the world. So are we willing? Are we willing to carry out God's program fully until the day He takes us home? May we take some time and tell Him we are? If not, be honest with Him and ask Him to make you want to get on board with whatever He tells you from here on out.

Lord, we call you Lord, and we want to mean it. We do mean it. As Your children, we are miserable when we put ourselves on the throne of our lives rather than surrender to You. Our commitment to You is that we will yield to Your Holy Spirit and watch carefully that we do not become obstinately set in our own purposes or opinions. For You are worthy! In Jesus's name, Amen.

WEEK 4 MEMORY VERSE:

"And He was saying to them all, 'If anyone wants to come with Me, he must deny himself, and take up his cross daily and follow Me'." Luke 9:23 (HCSB)

WEEK 4
DAY 3

"Surrender ~ The Pathway to Joy"

Only in God's economy can slavery and joy meet and rejoice hand in hand. Only in God's economy can surrender and dying to oneself, thus making Jesus preeminent in our lives, cause the greatest peace in our souls. Please turn to Deuteronomy 15:16-17. These are two short verses with some big lessons that I believe can parallel a New Testament believer's walk with the Lord in some amazing ways. It is written below for you also.

"It shall come about if he says to you, 'I will not go out from you,' because he loves you and your household, since he fares well with you; then you shall take an awl and pierce it through his ear into the door, and he shall be your servant forever."

The verses are speaking of a slave that wished to stay with their particular master for life. God gave Israel direction on how to go about making that happen. List below the three reasons the slave wished to stay where he was, realizing that freedom would never again be an option for them. This was willing servitude, the Bible says, *forever*.

The first reason given was that the slave loved the master. Why would we, as Christians, agree to willing servitude for all eternity to God through Jesus? Because we *love* God. We love Him because He first loved us! The reason for this ties into the third realization the slave had..."it was well with him." God pursued us, and when we realized how much He loved us (enough to die in our place and pay the penalty for our sins to be forever washed away) our souls cried out, "It is well with me!" We are taken care of now, we are not left as orphans, we have no need to fear or worry or stress. He has the entire universe under control *and He is for us*. Why would we ever want to leave His care? Because for a few short breaths it may be hard? Because there may be a time when we have to endure pain and suffering? During the hardest times, the hardest days, is it not then that His presence is the most powerful? Can we not trust that our Master's hand is for our good and our growth? We can. Take some time to tell the Lord, your Master and Lover that you will not go away from Him because you love Him and when you are with Him it is well with you. Thank Him for taking care of you and being faithful to you. Journal any thoughts below.

Now let's look at the middle reason why the servant wished to be a willing slave forever to this master...because he loved his master's *house*.

Psalm 26:8 says, "Lord, I have loved the habitation of Thy house, and the place where thine honour dwelleth."

Do we love the house of the Lord? We have to understand that the *people of God* are *included* in that phrase. Stop and ask yourself honestly, "Do I love the house of the Lord and God's people?" Maybe you are having a rough time at church right now. Maybe someone has hurt you badly. It is normal to feel that way sometimes (every relationship has issues that crop up at some point), but it is not OK to stay there. Bitterness *will* take root. If that is you, would you spend some time confessing it to the Lord and being willing to making that right? (It may be a process, but cooperate with the Spirit and start it now.) Like a gazelle running from a hunter, do whatever it takes to make that relationship right again. Get others involved to help you through it if needed. Find a godly counselor or mediator and stop the bleeding so God can heal it. Journal your thoughts below.

On the flip side, maybe you are in a position where you feel exactly like this slave. You can't imagine loving God more than you do right now and you are flourishing in the courts of your God. Praise Him for the quiet waters.

What about us? Do we love God? Have we tasted of His love and believe that it is "well" with us when we are in His care? Do we love His "house" (His church, His people)?

When we give ourselves wholly and completely to the will of God, we find joy. Not just hearing or reading His Word to us, but doing it. Because now we are in the center of His will and our souls can rest on the promises of His Word. The Bible says that God will work, "all things work together for good" in our lives. "ALL things?" Yes, even the most awful circumstances will be worked together for our good. Oh, but don't miss the second part of the verse (our part)..."to those who love Him and are called according to His purpose." So the blessing of God working all things together for good is for those who love Him.

We have a child who has a naturally compliant nature (is that possible?!). When I ask him to do things, his reaction is (I am not kidding), "Sure!" It is easy to bless that kind of obedience, it is natural to want to reward that. Although, even as I write this, I know of many times that God has been kind to me even in my rebellion. Out of His gracious hand I have received blessings even when I was going astray. So it is not a hard and fast rule that if you are obedient, blessing will *always and immediately* follow. It didn't for Joseph. It didn't for Daniel. It didn't for Jesus, or Paul, or Peter, or John. In fact, the Bible says that when we do all these things (obey the Lord and follow Him faithfully all the days of our lives) we should say, "we are unworthy students and have only done our duty." (Luke 17:10)

Some see blessing as materialistic things. Sometimes that is the case, but other times, there are more important blessings that we receive. The blessing of a problem being resolved or the blessing of a heart being changed. How about the blessing of a promise that even bad things will work together for good to those who love God. Those things are far better than a bigger house!

So what kind of joy does this complete surrender bring us?

1. *The joy of reward.* You know, laying our lives down at Jesus's feet is not *all* as ominus as "carrying a cross." I picture God like Fezziwig in "A Christmas Carol." He is a "Boss" worth working our hardest for. We are not doing it for nothing. We do not toil in vain. There are blessings here and in our lives to come.

Please read Luke 12:42-44.
What was the servant put in charge of while his Master was gone?

What was the servant put in charge of when the Master returned (because of his faithful stewardship)?

Please read Luke 19:12-19.
Notice in both of these parables, Jesus (Who is the Master and the Nobleman in each of these) gave His subjects (us!) certain responsibilities to do while He was "gone" (ie. At the right hand of the Father, which is right now). When those servants were faithful in completing the tasks He had given them, at His return (His second coming), He gives them authority and *more* responsibility (in heaven) than they had previously (here on earth)! Do we realize that this life is just a big "testing" ground in a way? Our faithfulness *here* will directly result in what our eternity will be like for us. *Heaven will not be the same for everyone.* Boy, that just lights a fire in me!! I just wonder if writing this study for instance, and being faithful in this "small" thing, will bring a special blessing that I will receive when I get there? According to these parables I will and so will you (if you listen and obey what God wants *you* to do)!

2. *The joy of our Master.* Our Father is a jovial God. Read Matthew 25:23. What does it say that the slave will enter into?

Make no mistake about it, God loves joy. Do you really think Jesus was stoic when He told Peter to go catch a fish for their tax money? (See Matthew 17:27.) What about when He told them to cast their nets on the other side and it brought fish so many that the boat almost sank? Don't you think that He laughed out loud with them when they came to shore? (See Luke 5:1-11.) Oh, He loves being God! He loves blessing us. His joy is supposed to be our joy and it comes with complete surrender and oneness with Him.

Please read Matthew 19:21-22. What was Jesus requiring of that young man?

The Bible is clear that how we deal with money is a heart issue. So money was not really what was being required of this man. *Everything* was being required of him. His whole heart would have to be engaged in Jesus and His will.

What was his countenance like when he refused to surrender all?

So it is with us. We were created to give ourselves to something greater, *Someone* greater. We can mask happiness with lots of other things, but when Jesus calls us to surrender and we refuse His call, something in us dies. How "hard" for the disciples to just immediately drop their nets and follow Jesus. I am sure it caused no little tiff among family members and no small gossip sessions from the neighbors. They themselves did not even understand all the implications of their decision, but when they saw the risen Jesus ascend to heaven and those tongues of fire come upon them in the upper room, I am sure the joy of their Master trumped anything they thought would have been hard to "surrender!"

So what is He calling you to surrender to Him, so you can fully enjoy the joy of Your Master? Anything external is just a sign of what He really wants internally, and when the external surrender is done because of our love for Him, be sure there is reward and fullness of joy to be had! Jot below what you believe He is telling you and share it with a trusted friend. Ask them to hold you accountable to doing what God has told you to do-go and do it quickly and completely.

My prayer Lord, is that You will clearly show us what Your plan is for us today. Make us to feel the joy You have when we want to love You through obedience. We want to know Your joy, it is our strength here on earth. In Jesus' name, amen.

WEEK 4 MEMORY VERSE:

"And He was saying to them all, 'If anyone wants to come with Me, he must deny himself, and take up his cross daily and follow Me'." Luke 9:23 (HCSB)

WEEK 4
DAY 4

"Surrender is a Continual Choice"

Week 4 Memory Verse:

"And He was saying to them all, 'If anyone wants to come with Me, he must deny himself, and take up his cross daily and follow Me'." Luke 9:23 (HCSB)

The memory verse is at the front of this lesson because it has a crucial point in regards to surrender. If you haven't figured it out from the title, it is the word "daily." We never "get it" in this life. We never "arrive." Either the wind of the Holy Spirit is blowing in our sails, or we are stagnant and drifting aimlessly. The good news is that this is true only in this life. The life to come will not have all the different things pulling at our allegiance and our surrender will not have to be a continual, conscious choice. It will just "be" without any distractions! Praise God!

God has shown over and over that He longs for a continual, intimate relationship with us. That is why He gave the Israelites manna one day at a time (except for the day before the Sabbath, see Exodus 16:21-22). Jesus called Himself the "manna from heaven". (See John 6:51.) It was a picture that we need Jesus as our *daily* portion. Just as a day without food or water can end up being pretty hairy, what are we like when we go a day without being nourished by the "Bread of Life" and drinking from the cup with "Living Water?" Shepherds go to their sheep every day to touch them and look them over. Once they have received that personal touch, they are on their merry way again.

I think, many times, we can look like this: Please read Revelation 3:16-17. What did Sardis look like without even knowing it?

God's desire for an intimate relationship is why He made the sacrificial system require *daily* sacrifices. Not all the sacrifices were for sin; some were for thanks, some were for fellowship, some were freewill offerings...a symbol of constant communion with the Lord. These sacrifices were done all day and even some things were required during the night hours. It is interesting that the reforms done during Israel's (and Judah's) dark times usually resulted in re-establishing the sacrificial system. Does this closeness with God in regular repentance, thanks, service, and joyful overflow sound like what we need?! These laws were put in place to point us to Christ. They were outward demonstrations of what we have established in our hearts because of Jesus's sacrifice. We are the temple of the Living God (1 Corinthians 3:16) which means that these "sacrifices" are still, in a spiritual sense, required of us. We are now the priests who are to carry out this ministry to the Lord (1 Peter 2:9). As it was then, it is still meant to be *continual*....daily. The Lord knows that this is hard to do on this side of heaven, so He gives us hefty support to keep on keepin' on.

Please read Galatians 6:8-9. Does any of that say something you needed to hear? Journal your thoughts.

Keep our eyes on the prize. Just like our lesson from yesterday, Paul writes about the eternal benefits of our choice to walk with the Lord continually here on this earth. Believing that He can and will speak personally to each of us makes this much easier! Think of how hard it would be if we just had to keep on with a "one-sided" relationship! He wants this constant connection with us, but we need to know that He is there keeping up His end of the bargain also. He has promised *never* to leave us (Matthew 27:20). He is faithful even when we are faithless (2 Timothy 2:13). He is ever-present to help us in trouble (Psalm 46:1). He will never let you be snatched out of His strong hand (John 10:28-29). The work He started in us He will continue until completion (Philippians 1:6).

Which of these do you need Him to be to you right now? He is all and more. Whatever you need. There is a chorus in a song about surrender that says, "Your love makes it worth it. Your love makes it worth it all." And it does. Listen, don't be ashamed because we need these things from Him as an incentive to surrender daily to Him. We should remember the verse, "We love because He first loved us" (1 John 4:19), and that is OK. All of our surrender stems from the fact that we have an awesome, loving God Who is worthy of it, worth it, and will help us do so. I super-spiritualize myself when I think that I don't need motivation in this life to live for the Lord. I do. Fortunately, He gives it.

Please read Phillipians 3:12-14 paying special attention to verse 13. What does Paul say about his past in verse 13?

This is a glorious truth. We can surrender today even what we did not surrender yesterday because yesterday is included in the phrase "forgetting what is behind!" His mercies are new every morning! I was just going to reference these verses, but I think they are perfect and need to be read here.

Please read Lamentations 3:22-24.

Don't live in condemnation and fail to surrender *today* because you are grieving over what you did not surrender *yesterday*! Ask for forgiveness and move on! I love to think that His compassions are new "every morning" (vs. 23) with the fact that a morning is dawning somewhere on the globe all (of our) day long! So this verse to me really means, "His compassions never fail, they are new every *moment!*"

What do you need to ask forgiveness for as a yesterday sin so that you can forget about it and follow Him wholeheartedly today?

Thank you for Your grace God. Your matchless grace that is so much greater than all our sin. Speak words of kindness and love to us today. Help our unbelief as we seek to surrender today even though we messed up just yesterday. You loved us while we were yet sinners, You love us still. We are so grateful for that! In Jesus's name, amen.

WEEK 4
DAY 5

"Because of Jesus"

This is our final lesson on surrender. The Lord took me to a verse that may be familiar to some of you, but I believe He wants us to look at it with new eyes. The Amplified version is a great translation for this particular lesson.

"I appeal to you therefore brethren, and beg of you in view of [all] the mercies of God, to make a decisive dedication of your bodies [presenting all your members and faculties] as a living sacrifice, holy (devoted, consecrated) and well pleasing to God, which is your reasonable (rational, intelligent) service and spiritual worship." Romans 12:1 (AMP)

Let's dissect this.

"I appeal to you brethren, and beg of you..." The word for "appeal" and "beg" in this verse literally means, "to call to one's side or aid." Paul was not asking the church at Rome to do something that he had not done. He was begging them strongly to do what he was also doing, to come alongside of him so they could do this surrender thing together. Hopefully a thread that has been woven in this study so far is the importance of the Body of Christ coming together. As you encourage me in my daily walk with Christ, I encourage you back. Two are better than one and a strand of three cords is not easily broken. (Ecclesiastes 4:9a,12b my paraphrase)

Please read the verse again. Because of what reason were they to present themselves as a living sacrifice to God?

Spiros Zodhiates (editor of the Key Word Greek and Hebrew Study Bible) says of Romans, "it is by far the most comprehensive statement of the full meaning of the cross of Christ." So I am going to take some liberty to say what I think Paul was saying in Romans 12:1. "Let all the mercies we have received because of Jesus, (and I have outlined them for you in the first 11 chapters of this letter) cause you to make a decision to surrender everything you are, inside and out, to God."

Let's look at just *some* of the mercies of God that are our motivation for these rational acts of worship that God desires of us. Remember, these lessons are to get our hearts in a place that is willing to say, "Sure!" to whatever the Lord would tell/lead us to do. God does not require our "blind" obedience. He may not give us reasons right away as to *why* He is telling us to do such and such, but He gives us plenty of reasons as to *why we can trust Him and do it anyway.*

One of the reasons that a Shepherd spends a lot of time in the midst of the sheep just talking to them is so that they can learn to trust him. They not only learn his voice, but they connect it with the care and the provision he demonstrates to them day after day. In other words, "blind faith" is for the birds! We have plenty of reasons to say "Yes" to God even if we don't understand the full reasons for why He is asking. His constant care and provision for us thus far in our lives is reason enough to trust Him today and tomorrow! Just for fun, I want to start in Romans chapter 1 and pick some mercies out of each chapter. First I want to pray just to make sure that the Holy Spirit has the freedom to really open our eyes to these mercies. I don't want to just read them to read them. I want them to cause us to exult in what the Lord has done for us!

Holy Spirit, by Your great power, cause us to really see these mercies for what they are. Cause them also to do what they are supposed to do and that is to give us every reason to fully surrender to God as a well-pleasing act of worship. In Jesus' name, amen.

By His great mercy: we are called beloved. Romans 1:7
By His great mercy: we have received the riches of His kindness. Romans 2:4
By His great mercy: we are justified through the redemption found in Jesus, though we were unrighteous sinners. Romans 3:23-24
By His great mercy: our lawless deeds will not be taken into account! Romans 4:7-8
By His great mercy: our hope in God will *not ever* disappoint us (my emphasis). Romans 5:5
By His great mercy: we are, through Christ's blood, saved from the wrath of God. Romans 5:9
By His great mercy: we will be raised from the dead and changed into the likeness of Christ. Romans 6:5
By His great mercy: this wretched body of death is set free! Romans 7:24-25
By His great mercy: we have received a spirit of adoption rather than fear. Romans 8:15
By His great mercy: we can call God our "Daddy." Romans 8:15
By His great mercy: we who were not His people, are now His people. Romans 9:25
By His great mercy: there are abounding riches for all who call upon Him. Romans 10:12
By His great mercy: whoever will call upon His name will be allowed to be saved. Romans 10:13
By His great mercy: we are under grace rather than under works. Romans 11:6

Praise God! The Psalmist cries, "His mercies endure forever!" Our God is not fickle in His divvying out of mercy. If we are His children, we are under a covenant of mercy that endures forever! So in light of all these spectacular mercies that we take for granted most days, we are to make a "decisive dedication of our bodies as a living sacrifice." I love that the Amplified Bible says "our bodies" include "all our members and faculties." That means any of our abilities, our talents, memory, reason etc. are to be offered up to God to use for His purposes. Our hands and feet and whole being are to be holy (set apart) for whatever He desires! As I have mentioned before, it would be fine for God to require all of this from us with *nothing* to be gained in return, but look at what happens...we can be "well-pleasing" to God.

God can be pleased. Let that sink in for a moment. Have you ever had anyone cross your path that was impossible to please? Maybe it was a close, consistent influence in your life. Well, let me tell you somethin'—**God** is not like that! When we are pleased with someone, we have a fond affection for him or her. We smile when we think of them. We even go so far as to rejoice over them, don't we? I think, of course, about when my children please me with their obedience and when they surrender themselves willingly to what I am asking of them. Do I rejoice over them? You bet I do! My heart nearly bursts with pleasure over them...don't put God in an unemotional box or worse yet — a box of anger or aloofness towards you! In most movies, where Jesus is portrayed, He is rather somber and serious most of the time. Sometimes I just want to jump up and shout, "Where is the overflowing joy?!" I know God is not somber and serious all the time because I have felt His presence in me. This pleasure of God is felt in His presence, which is where we would be if we were standing constantly before Him as a "living sacrifice." Let yourself feel His joy and love over you as you surrender to Him. Don't let the enemy snatch that away.

Let's look at the last couple of phrases. What is "reasonable" defined as in the Amplified Bible?

In light of all that Christ has done for us and all the blessings of knowing God now and in heaven, it is completely rational to lay ourselves down on the altar. Understanding our need for surrender is necessary in order to hear God with the intent to obey. We might get all excited to hear Him, but the obedience part is the other side to the coin. If I am a surrendered servant, the obedience aspect is not as difficult. Not only is it rational (yes, our faith is a *rational* faith), it is *intelligent* for us to do this! It is not smart to kick against the goads, as Paul reminds us in Acts 26:14. It is very wise to give ourselves fully to God, who has nothing but complete and utter love for us in His heart. To the God who wants to bless us and extend all-powerful grace to us and change us from dead-in-sin people to alive-in-Him! He knows that it will fill us to the fullest measure to let this verse come to life in us so I pray it will. In my life and yours. Take some time to pray Romans 12:1 over yourself and someone else today. Blessings!

WEEK 4 MEMORY VERSE:

"And He was saying to them all,
'If anyone wants to come with Me,
he must deny himself, and take up his cross daily
and follow Me'." Luke 9:23 (HCSB)

WEEK 5
DAY 1

"Faith Like a Mustard Seed"

How strong do you believe your "faith" is in general? Not your faith based on your wavering emotions, but deep down underneath it all, what kind of faith do you believe you have? Journal your thoughts below.

Read Matthew 17:20. What does Jesus say that just a little bit of faith will do?

Some of us may have heard this verse many times but I want to share an insight the Lord gave me once when I was struggling with how "small" my faith was. This is a conversation I had with the Lord about it.

Me- "But Lord, my faith is smaller than a mustard seed."
Him- "My child, within that tiny mustard seed is *every element needed* for that seed to grow into one of the largest garden plants. It only means that your faith needs to grow, not that the gift is not there or is only there in part."

I personally had never thought of that before. That within the seed, already, is *every element needed* for the large tree. So even if our faith is as small as a mustard seed (about the size of the head of a pin), it has everything already needed to "move the mountain!" As we water our faith (with the Word), grow in the grace and knowledge of Christ (the Light of the Son), and obey the Holy Spirit's guidance (the wind or air that all plants need), our faith will continue to grow until others can even come and take refuge in our "branches." (Matthew 13:31-32)

What do you believe "mountains" may represent in this verse?

Are you facing any "mountains" in your life? Any "giants?" (See 1 Samuel 17.) So what do we do with this verse? I asked my husband that the other day about this verse and he said, "We believe it!" I am not aiming at an unbalanced view of a "mountain" being the need for a Lexus rather than a Corolla. In context, Jesus was teaching this in regards to overcoming the enemy. The disciples had been unable to cast out a demon and Jesus said that it was because of the "littleness of their faith." (Matthew 17:20a) Isn't a big part of life asking Him to answer our requests regarding the "mountains" we face? How is our faith in believing they can be "cast into the sea" by our prayers?

Tomorrow we are going to discuss what role our faith plays in answered prayer, but for now would you write out any and all "mountains" that you are facing at the moment?

I can remember (and will never forget) one particular mountain that loomed over me so tall that I could barely make it from day to day. Hardly a moment went by without my crying out to the Lord about it. It was a season of my life that lasted almost two full years. God does not waste any time or thing that we go through and I want to leave you with this encouragement. It was a word the Lord gave me in regards to what I was facing and maybe it will speak to you also as you cry out to the Lord about your "mountains" this week. It is found in Zechariah 4:7a.

> "What are you, mighty mountain?
> Before (insert your name here)
> you will become level ground."

My mountain did become level ground under my feet. I grabbed hold of this verse with all the (little) faith I had and God answered my prayers. Now, would you join me in lifting our "mountains" up to the Lord with fresh confidence that God desires to answer your requests? Thank Him for this desire and do whatever it takes to nurture your faith (no matter how small) and make it bigger! It pleases Him for His people to have BIG faith! The more we hear from God and the more we hear Him answer us and watch Him work on our behalf, the more our faith will grow if we let it. Our part is to believe Him, remember each thing that He does for us, and face the next mountain by speaking the previous victory over it...not start at square one in our faith every time a new mountain comes up!

In closing, I have seen three different ways that God can handle our mountains as we pray about them. They can either be moved, leveled, or climbed. Moved, meaning thrown into the sea so as to not have to deal with it again. Leveled, meaning God just flattens it as though it was not there in the first place. Or climbed. My mountain that I was referring to, was climbed. The "thing", the mountain, was still there, but God allowed me to conquer it. It was under my feet, not looming over my head anymore. I was able to enjoy the freedom of the view from the high place, and now I knew the path to the top if I ever needed to conquer it again. Whatever way He does it, I know that it is not His desire for His children to be caught up in the anxiety, anger, or unbelief that mountains have the potential to cause. He wants us to, through prayer, put Him in the position to get rid of them for us one way or another. Then we will have no room for boasting in anything but Him. I will be praying for you, that even this week your "mountains" will be cast into the sea!

Lord, this mountain that I am facing is more than I know what to do with. As I order my prayers to You and wait on You to subdue it, will You keep my mind at peace and my faith strong? I believe that You love me and that You are going to show me the way past this because You are a faithful God! Thank You Jesus, Amen.

WEEK 5 MEMORY VERSE:

"And we receive from Him whatever we ask, because we [watchfully] obey His orders [observe His suggestions and injunctions, follow His plan for us] and [habitually] practice what is pleasing to Him.

1 John 3:22 (AMP)

WEEK 5
DAY 2

"Faith and Answered Prayer"

This is where it can get sticky. We saw yesterday that the disciples were unable to do a work of God (it was, in essence, an unanswered prayer) because of their lack of faith. There were times in Jesus's ministry when He did not do many miracles because of their lack of faith (Matthew 13:58 NIV). Let's read some other examples where faith had something to do with prayers being answered.

Read Matthew 9:28-30. What were the men "praying for"?

What did Jesus say was a catalyst in their healing?

How about Luke 5:18-20? What caught the attention of Jesus in this story?

There are a myriad of examples where faith was said to be an intricate part of prayers being answered. So it is with us. Growing up in more so-called "conservative" churches, I have found there is not much teaching on this aspect of receiving from God according to our faith. We know that any truth can be taken to a false extreme and I hope to present this truth in its balanced, Biblical form. I personally need to have more faith-filled confidence in the One to Whom I am praying! I need to come to Him more boldly and expectantly! Even so, we still need to come with plenty of room for God's sovereignty. Oh, but I don't let that stop us from petitioning with fervor and persistence! He told us to pray in these ways.

What does James 1:5-8 say about faith in regards to answered prayer?

Would you be willing to read this same passage again in the Amplified Version? It is written out for you; I just love how it really brings definition to what this "double-minded" man looks like.

James 1:5-8 (Amp) "If any of you is deficient in wisdom, let him ask of the giving God [Who gives] to everyone liberally and ungrudgingly, without reproaching or faultfinding, and it will be given him. Only it must be in faith that he asks with no wavering (no hesitating, no doubting). For the one who wavers (hesitates, doubts) is like the billowing surge out at sea that is blown hither and thither and tossed by the wind. For truly, let not such a person imagine that he will receive anything [he asks for] from the Lord, [For being as he is] a man of two minds (hesitating, dubious, irresolute), [he is] unstable and unreliable and uncertain about everything [he thinks, feels, decides]."

A major aspect of needing to hear God's voice, is our need for His wisdom in our lives. We need to know how to handle situations and relationships supernaturally. So one thing that we can petition Him for and *know* we will get an answer for, is His wisdom. Some petitions we have are left up to His mysterious sovereignty, still some are answered exactly how we prayed for them, but His wisdom is *guaranteed* for those who seek it with a faith-filled heart. How can we ask for His wisdom if we don't believe He speaks? Who are we waiting for an answer from and how do we expect Him to answer it, if we don't believe God would talk to us or supernaturally intervene in our lives in a way that we know that it is Him? So James makes it very clear: you will not receive anything from God if you doubt (ie. continually waffling back and forth especially if He is making His will to you very clear).

Have you ever been around a person described like the one at the end of these verses? I have been that person before and I have seen others in such a state. Where everything is a confusing issue in their lives even if everyone around them is giving them sound, godly counsel to make good decisions. It'll drive a person crazy. I've driven myself crazy at times! So it *does* take faith to receive from God because faith asks God for an answer, believes that He will give it, and acts upon it when the answer comes!

This is a good time to ask yourself what "camp" do you fall into? The camp that throws up prayers hoping that God might turn and notice them one day but not really expecting an answer? Then move toward the Biblical exhortation that tells us to come to the throne of grace boldly to receive the help we need.

Are you of the "camp" that doesn't leave room for God's sovereignty and sets yourself up for disappointment because you believe that *everything* you ask for you'll receive, if you just have enough faith? Which also leaves those watching a bit confused because God didn't work it out exactly the way you petitioned for it to happen, although He was "supposed" to. This is where we pray with all our might, but in the end we trust His loving hand to do what is best.

The Lord brought a really good illustration to mind while I was meditating on this topic.

Please read 2 Samuel 12:13-23.

Here is an instance where David sought the Lord with all faith hoping that God would be merciful and spare the child, but he left it in the hands of God's sovereignty. He also prayed fervently and persistently. Sadly, the child died, but notice how David responded to the Lord's sovereign decision. In verse 20, he arose and worshiped. So it should be with us. With all faith, we seek and cry out expectantly waiting for our God to answer! Faith gets His attention. Faith causes Him to move on our behalf. But the answer is still from the Lord and we can rest our souls in that. So let's take our faith to a new level as we seek Him and see what He does! Without hesitation, I believe He desires to come to our aid and work supernatural deeds in our lives to His glory!

Father, You are sovereign, we know that. Yet You allow us to be your children through Jesus and even come to You with our petitions. May we believe that You desire to answer our prayers with Your wisdom and guidance even if the outcome is not what we thought we wanted. You know what is best and although we are to pray with fervency and confidence, You are still the One in control and we trust Your love. Thank You for tearing the veil and allowing us total access to You through Jesus we pray, Amen.

WEEK 5 MEMORY VERSE:

"And we receive from Him whatever we ask, because we [watchfully] obey His orders [observe His suggestions and injunctions, follow His plan for us] and [habitually] practice what is pleasing to Him.

1 John 3:22 (AMP)

Week 5
Day 3

"Changing the Mind of God"

What an interesting lesson this is. So far this week we have learned that even a little bit of faith can move mountains and that faith is needed for us to receive anything from God. How would it change our prayer life if we thought that our petitions could actually cause God to change His mind? I think it would open up a whole new level of my relationship with Him if I knew that He would actually listen to me and take *my* prayers into account as He ordered the universe! Like yesterday, we are going to look up lots of examples of what the *Word* has to say about this subject, so let's get our Bibles and start reading!

The first example we are going to study is found in 2 Kings 20:1-6. Jot down your first thoughts about this passage below.

How peculiar. I mean, what did Isaiah think about having to turn right back around and give a "word" completely opposite of what he had just given? Here is a question for thought…Do you think that some things in our lives could be altered if only we would fervently pray about them?

This next passage is actually one that the Lord gave me recently when I was praying about something. It is in Amos chapter 7. Please read verses 1-6. What did God change His mind about in this passage?

Let's look at just one more. Exodus 32:11-14.
Did you notice a common thread in these passages that seemed to cause God to change His mind? Write your thoughts below.

The two things that seem to get the Lord's attention and cause Him to relent, especially of calamity, are:
1. Man's intercession.
2. Man's repentance.

Wow. Even a "word" declared by God as something that was *going to happen*, changed when *man* repented and cried out to God for it not to be so. Have you ever thought about the fact that most prophecy in the Old Testament gives a conditional decree depending on the response of man? I would have balked at this teaching back in my college days getting my Bible degree. But now, after many more years of studying the Scriptures and living life with Him, I am more in awe of the *mystery* that surrounds God's interactions with us. How can He be completely sovereign, with His every desire and purpose being able to stand, while relenting and responding to mere men and women? I do not know this side of heaven. But I am thankful for it. I am thankful that my fate is not sealed for doom if I choose to repent and intercede on behalf of myself and others! I am thankful that God is a God of pity and that He desires to relent of the calamity He is morally bound to perform when we continue in our wicked ways! What fear of Him and love for Him should well up inside of us at this understanding! Especially when we read a verse like Jeremiah 15:6 which says, "You who have forsaken Me," declares the Lord, "You keep going backward, so I will stretch out my hand against you and destroy you; I am tired of relenting!" (NASB)

We do not want this to be God's attitude towards us! There was a time when I received a "word" similar to this from the Lord. He was getting fed up with me. His desire was not to consume me, but my sinful patterns had to change. The only prayer He desired me to pray was, "Will You forgive me and do whatever it takes to change me?" I am so thankful for His endless grace that picked me up yet once again as I repented and turned to Him again. Be assured that if you are surrendered to God and living a life pleasing to Him, your prayers carry weight. The prayers of the righteous are a pleasing aroma to Him. What a joy to know that He lets us join Him in this earthly life by hearing our prayers and even, at times, changing His mind to do what we ask of Him! I feel like a broken record, but fervent, faith-filled prayers catch the heart of God. What if, I mean what *if*, God is staying His hand on an issue in our lives due to the lack of prayer about it on our part?

Who or what situation in your life needs your intercession and repentance? If you are comfortable doing so, write about it below and jot a prayer to the Lord about it. Hopefully your prayer will be brought forth with new fervor and faith and expectancy! May God continue to reveal Himself to you in mighty, amazing ways.

Week 5 Memory Verse:

"And we receive from Him whatever we ask, because we [watchfully] obey His orders [observe His suggestions and injunctions, follow His plan for us] and [habitually] practice what is pleasing to Him.

1 John 3:22 (AMP)

WEEK 5
DAY 4

"Sin vs. Answered Prayer"

Our discussion this week is centered around what God says about answered prayer. I think it is fair to say that it is something we, as Believers, desire in our walks with the Lord. We pray at least *hoping* that things will turn out as we desire, but is there anything that can keep us from experiencing answers to our prayers?

Please read the Amplified Bible's translation of 1 Peter 3:7 below. What does it say about prayer in this verse?

"In the same way you married men should live considerately with [your wives], with an [a]intelligent recognition [of the marriage relation], honoring the woman as [physically] the weaker, but [realizing that you] are joint heirs of the grace (God's unmerited favor) of life, in order that your prayers may not be hindered and cut off. [Otherwise you cannot pray effectively.]"

Before we think that it is all on our husbands (if you are married), read also Psalm 66:17-18. What does it say will hinder *us* from being heard by God?

Mark 11:25 says that if we stand praying, we need to forgive whatever we have against someone else so that we can be forgiven of God. So there is a direct relation to answered prayers or God hearing our prayers and the state of our hearts. There is also a correlation to God hearing our prayers and the state of our relationships with other people. Sound familiar? Jesus said the two greatest commandments were to "Love God and love our neighbors." (Luke 10:26-28) So to enjoy this free, unhindered, powerful prayer life, we must be sure these two things are in place.

So ask the Lord right now, "Is there anything I have in my heart against You that would keep You from hearing my prayers?" Journal your thoughts below.

Whether there is a whole list of things He brought to mind, or nothing at the moment, be assured that if we confess, He is faithful and just to forgive. In fact, He is bound to His Word to perform this act of forgiveness! We are clean and holy in Christ. Now on to part two.

"Lord, is there any sin or unforgiveness (on my part) in my relationships with others that would keep you from hearing my prayers?" Journal your thoughts below.

As hard as it may be on the front side, do whatever He leads you to do in order to make those relationships right. You are responsible for your part. Not God's and not theirs. You are to forgive whatever greivances you have against another. You are responsible for being willing for the Holy Spirit to soften your heart so that the relationship can be restored. But you do not have the power to make all of that happen, or make the other person do what you want them to do. It will bring tremendous peace to your soul even if the other person is not willing to reconcile. For you will be right with the Lord and, as much as it depends on you, your relationships with others will be at peace.

Now, there should be nothing hindering our prayers because we are keeping His commandments and (habitually) doing those things which are pleasing in His sight (see verse below). So in faith I can pray with all my heart knowing that I have the listening ear of the God of the universe! And if we have His ear, then we can be assured that He stands ready to answer!

WEEK 5 MEMORY VERSE:

"And we receive from Him whatever we ask, because we [watchfully] obey His orders [observe His suggestions and injunctions, follow His plan for us] and [habitually] practice what is pleasing to Him.
1 John 3:22 (AMP)

WEEK 5
DAY 5

"What are we asking for?"

So faith matters, the state of our heart matters, the state of our relationships matter...does answered prayer depend on what we pray for? Is God "required" to give us the big house, perfect health, and a carefree, tribulation-less life? For the most part, I think we would agree that the answer to those questions is "No". But are there prayers that *will not* be answered by God?

Our answer is found in James 4:2-3. As you read it, list below the things that keep us from getting what we ask of God.

Did you notice that one of the first reasons we "do not have" is because "we do not ask?" Have you ever done that? Moaned and groaned about your circumstances, even told others that you hoped that God would work on your behalf, but failed to ask **Him** for it? Oh, I have. I have mulled things around in my mind with the thought that only God could change it, but I did not turn my thoughts to Him and actually cry out to Him about it! Remember, God is after intimacy with us, so just thinking about it is not enough.

Hopefully you were able to see that we fail to receive because we ask with wrong motives. What kind of motives does God call evil and selfish? Let's read Philippians 2:3 in the Amplified Version.

"Do nothing from factional motives [through contentiousness, strife, selfishness, or for unworthy ends] or prompted by conceit and empty arrogance. Instead, in the true spirit of humility (lowliness of mind) let each regard the others as better than and superior to himself [thinking more highly of one another than you do of yourselves]."

From that, what can we define selfish, evil motives as?

Are any of those true in our lives? Have I been motivated by the desire to be seen as "right" when I am praying? Am I asking for things that lead to "unworthy ends"? Or do my prayers come from the desire to elevate others and put them before myself? Do our cries for more money come from our desire to go to Disney World or to have more to give to others in need? Hopefully the balance to that question is already understood…family vacations are fine, but are we as generous with others as we are with ourselves? Maybe if this were the case, we would see more of our prayers answered. Especially if the Lord knew that we want to receive from Him so that we can be a blessing to others.

This does not just have to do with our finances. It also deals with our jealousy of the status another person may have, how they look physically, what we view their family life like, anything we desire for our own selfish pleasures. Maybe to be "known" like them, or to be "happy" like them. We must remember that it is more blessed to give than to receive and we receive so that we can share with others. So as we ask things of God, may it be with pure motives that seek to receive so that we may have something to give away. A really neat example of this is found in Luke 11:5-8. Please read it and answer the questions below.

What was the man asking his friend for?

Why did he need them?

(There's a really good point coming, stay with me!)
Did he get what he was asking for?

I heard an amazing sermon on this passage and the Pastor talked about how there was no greater joy than receiving from heaven in order to have enough to share. The man was not asking for the bread for himself! He was asking for it so that he would have something to share! This is a sign of maturity growing in a believer. Do we ask amiss when all our requests are "us" centered? Would we begin to see more of our prayers answered if we were knocking down heaven's door in order that *others* could have the blessings we so desire for ourselves? A marvelous kingdom truth is that *we* get to share in the same joy we give away! So I hope this lesson changes what we are asking God for. "God give me a word for so and so, to encourage her in her time of distress." "God, would you give us the money to be able to provide them with the winter coats their kids need?" This difference would begin to change the world...and us.

Father, may we watch our prayers turn from self-centered to others-centered. Make us more aware of the needs around us. May we not be overwhelmed when we see all the needs for You have given us Your Holy Spirit to show us which one(s) we personally are supposed to meet. Thank You for the storehouse of power and blessings You stand ready to give us as we turn to a hurting, lost world and hurting brothers and sisters in order to give away what we have so freely received. Bless Your holy name! In Jesus we pray, Amen.

Week 5 Memory Verse:

"And we receive from Him whatever we ask, because we [watchfully] obey His orders [observe His suggestions and injunctions, follow His plan for us] and [habitually] practice what is pleasing to Him.
1 John 3:22 (AMP)

WEEK 6
DAY 1

"All Wrapped up in Love"

The title of this lesson is the overarching theme for this last week. Love is the greatest sum of all the commandments and the prophets. Love is what sets us apart as Christians. God's agape love. Unconditional, ever-flowing, one-sided (it doesn't need us to love back, it is just always there) love. Only through the Holy Spirit, Who I hope you have gotten to know better in the last few weeks, can we love like this. Yesterday's lesson moved us from just hearing from God for ourselves, but seeking and hearing from God for other people. This week we are going to talk about how that specifically looks and how to do that in the love and power of the Holy Spirit.

Three times Jesus asked Peter if he loved Him and after each affirmative answer Peter gave, there was a request that Peter would have to obey. So it is with us. God is asking us, individually, "Do you love Me?" If we say "yes" then we need to know that close behind that "yes" is a unique task He is calling us to do for Him.

Read John 21:15-17. What commands did Jesus give Peter after hearing him affirm his love for Him?

I am not advocating that all of our "callings" will look the same. I am advocating that, like Peter, our love for Jesus will move us into service for others. We need to hear from Him individually as to what that would be. All we need to do is affirm our love for Him; He will cast the specific vision He has for our lives. Peter was called to feed His sheep and tend His lambs. This week of our homework is going to take us outside of ourselves to hear what God has to say to us in regards to how He wants to use us for other people. There is power, motivation, joy, and eternal fruit from seeing and implementing the unique vision that God has for each of our lives. Even if you feel like you know what that vision looks like overall, it takes hearing from Him on an ongoing basis as to how that fleshes itself out everyday.

Please read Proverbs 29:18. What does it say happens when there is no vision?

Our families perish, our marriages perish, our souls perish. We may still be alive and breathing, but there is no real "life" when Jesus has not breathed His vision for us into us. Memories of an 11-year personal drought bring tears to my eyes as I write this. My famine, my wilderness wanderings, were partly God's sovereignty and training and partly my own disobedience of not walking in the calling He had for me. What a desolate time! What drudgery! Ugghhh. I don't ever want to go back there and by God's grace and my obedience, I won't. Let's look at what Proverbs 29:18 says in the original language. I am using the NASB version.

"Where there is no vision, the people are unrestrained, but happy is he who keeps the law."

Vision~ This is the same word used in week two. It is a mental sight, a dream, a vision, a prophecy. A vision comes to us as *given by God*. It means that I don't need to conjure up something that I think would be good to do for Him, I just need to seek Him and receive my tasks from Him.

Unrestrained~ undisciplined, ignored, exposed, unruly, to become lawless. It carries the sense of letting something slip through our fingers by ignoring an opportunity.

Wow. Take that to the Motherhood bank and deposit it! How sensitive my children are to the fact that I don't have a "vision" for the day! I "expose" them when I am not covering them with order and discipline and it makes them unruly! I have proved this verse in my own home. Now apply it to the purposes you have been created to fulfill in the Kingdom of God. Apply it to your role as a wife if you are married. If we do not have a vision for each of these things, they will be hindered from being all they can be.

Our pastor said something that God has used mightily in my life in regards to having a vision. He said, "aim determines direction." If we have no aim, we have no direction, if we do not have goals, be assured, we will go nowhere fast. So today, we are going to pray for God's vision for our lives. Not for the sake of focusing on ourselves, but to respond to a calling that would lead us into greater discipline for the service of others. Jesus is saying, "Do you love Me? Then….."

I understand that these prayers may not be fully answered in 5 minutes, but we need journal what we feel like He gives us immediately, then keep our eyes open as He might expound on it later. He may just give you a few ways to tweak and make better what you are already doing. He may think you are doing awesome and just encourage you to keep going! At the very least, let it motivate you to serve in these areas with all your heart again today!

Lord, please give me a vision, from You, for my role as a wife (if you are married).

Lord, please give me a vision, from You, for my role as a mother (if you have children).

Lord, please give me a vision, from You, for my role as a servant in Your Kingdom (if you are saved).

Be assured that He is waiting to speak to you about these things! Jesus said that "the harvest is plentiful but the laborers are few." That means there is much work to be done and that there is a place for you and I to help as He has uniquely created us to do. As we seek to hear and implement these things, here is a verse that constantly motivates me:

Week 6 Memory Verse:

"Therefore, my dear brothers and sisters, stand firm.
Let nothing move you.
Always give yourselves fully to the work of the Lord,
because you know that your labor in the Lord is not in vain."
1 Corinthians 15:58 (NIV)

Lord, give us ears to hear the specific purposes You have put us on this earth for. May we not lose another day floundering or unaware of the good deeds Your Holy Spirit wants us to do today. Not only as we try to walk in those, show us an overall vision for our lives that will motivate us to our dying day. Thank You for the part You created each of us to play, may we seek what that is with all our hearts and walk in fervent obedience to it so that we may declare that we have fought the good fight and finished the race well! In Jesus' name, Amen.

WEEK 6
DAY 2

"Poured Out as a Drink Offering..."

The Bible says, "it is more blessed to give than to receive." (Acts 20:35) This week, as we look beyond hearing from God and experiencing Him just for ourselves, I hope that this verse rings true in your life in a powerful way. There is nothing like feeling the power of God flow through us for the sake of another. It will spend us, it will pour us out until we wonder if we can do anymore, but then God comes right behind and fills us up again to continue to do His will.

Twice the Apostle Paul used the phrase that he has been "poured out as a drink offering." Once in Phillippians 2:17 and again in 2 Timothy 4:6. The drink offering was an offering of *joy* (strong, sweet wine) poured over the sweet savour offerings. One sweet savour offering was called the burnt offering which symbolized Jesus' death in respect to God's pleasure in His (Jesus) complete obedience to His will. The other offering was the meal offering which symbolized Jesus's perfect life from birth to death. The peace offering, is Jesus' work and reward of bringing His created beings back into fellowship with God through His death.

The drink offering was poured over the top of these to signify the utter joy of God over the beautiful work that Christ performed in obedience to God and on our behalf!

Please read Isaiah 53:10a given below.

"But the Lord was pleased to crush Him, putting Him to grief; if He would render Himself as a guilt offering..."

What does it say God felt while Jesus was being made a guilt offering for us?

One of the instances for which Paul used the analogy of the drink offering in his own life was when he was in prison. The other time was when he sensed that he was about to leave this world and be martyred. How could he use the symbol of a drink offering in those two dreadful instances? For the drink offering was *only* to be used as an offering of joy, it was not to be used on either the sin or trespass offerings which symbolized Christ's sufferings. Suffering does not please God. He was not joyful when Christ was crying out over His being separated from His Father for the first time in all eternity past while bearing our hideous sins. God, and Paul, were joyful at what the work *accomplished*.

So when we are pouring ourselves out because God has led us to serve another and it takes us places we didn't want to go and more of us than we wanted to give, we must look ahead to what it *accomplishes*. We must remember that God is only concerned with the "here and now" as it effects eternity. There is always a bigger picture and we can rejoice in being poured out, knowing that if God has told us to do so, we have just been more blessed than the one who received our ministry. What we hear from God for our own lives is good and necessary, but hearing from God to be poured out for another is better and is a sweet aroma to the Father.

In our prayer time, let's thank God for *desiring* to use us in ways that would please Him and bring Him glory. When you desire something, you really want it. I don't use that word lightly. God really, really wants us to jump on board and bear eternal fruit for His name! He has good works already marked out for us to do; our job is to listen and obey. Now think about that particular situation/person who is on your mind, to whom you need to be ministering. (If you can't think of anyone, start by asking Him to show you someone who needs some ministering. He will.) Ask Him to give you more love and knowledge and discernment about how you could be a drink offering for Him through that situation.

I have felt at times as though I wanted to give up. Pouring yourself out for others can make you very tired. It can leave you feeling tired emotionally, physically, and financially. But no greater love has anyone than this, but that he lay down his life for his friends. Let's ask God for a fresh filling of His Spirit to faithfully complete whatever "work" He has called us to. Our labor for the Lord is not in vain. Also, do not grow weary in doing good for at the proper time you will reap a harvest if you do not give up! One of the passages that encourages me when I am at the point of exhaustion is Psalm 23.

Please read verses 1-3. Notice that the Shepherd (the Lord) makes us to lie down in green pastures. That means that we give it all we've got and He knows exactly when we need to lie down and rest and we look to Him for that. Like a good coach to an Olympic athlete, He pushes me farther than I think I can go. I have felt so exhausted that I literally cried when serving others, but He was training me. He was in control of when the green pastures needed to be there. The quiet waters need to come every once in a while when needed, just don't expect them to be the norm when you are following Jesus. Paul endured a lot of sleepless nights and physical exhaustion during his ministry here on earth (see 2 Corinthians 11:23-33), but as the memory verse for this week states, "your labor for the Lord is not in vain!"

Father, we have said that we will follow You, keep us faithful when it gets tiring and hard. Help us to use the refreshment that You have provided to us through our local churches and godly friends to keep us going when we don't think we can go another step. May Your refreshment be sweet and gratefully received by us. Thank You Jesus. Amen.

WEEK 6 MEMORY VERSE:

"Therefore, my dear brothers and sisters, stand firm. Let nothing move you. Always give yourselves fully to the work of the Lord, because you know that your labor in the Lord is not in vain."

1 Corinthians 15:58 (NIV)

WEEK 6
DAY 3

"Feeling a bit like Jonah"

OK, so we don't want to do it. He has given us some direction, some person, some task, and we flat-out-don't-want-to. What do we do then? Romans 15:4 says that, "whatever things were written before were written for our learning." (NKJV) So we know that we don't want to run like Jonah, 'cause God can get us! We know we don't want to whine like the Israelites during the wilderness wanderings because God had severe consequences for that also. One misunderstanding I lived half my Christian life thinking was at this crossroads right here. You know what I thought? That *I* had to change my heart and mind about it. It is only the Spirit in us that can make us want to do anything that God says. What makes me think that starting in the Spirit I can "roll up my sleeves" and, by my flesh, change my own heart about something? It is very liberating to know that I don't have to! So what *can* I do so that I don't obstinately disobey, or whine and lose the "promised land" He is trying to give me? Here are steps that have been extremely helpful to me.

1. Tell Him everything you are thinking and feeling. Even write it out. Be c o m p l e t e l y honest.

2. Confess to Him that you know His way is best and that you are willing for Him to change your heart. (Note: You don't have to have a heart change at this point, but you do have to be *willing* for Him to make you want to do His will.)

3. Begin taking steps of obedience in faith, dying to yourself, and He will bring your emotions around.

Sometimes I have to do these steps over before I finally allow Him to get a hold of me, but I do always try my best to be *willing* to be changed. If there is ever something that I am really hard-hearted about and I don't even want to be willing to be changed on, I take that as a 9-1-1 to my close friends and ask them to start praying for me! That is a dangerous place to play and I don't like to be there. But I admit that I get there sometimes. Even so, these steps have proven very effective in my short little life so far and I know that it will prove true for you also! There is not a time that I can remember where the Holy Spirit has not stepped in the gap and helped me do God's will, not because I *wanted* to, but because deep down I wanted His will for my life. Even if that meant dying to self and being led where I didn't want to go.

One more example of being led where you don't want to go but still moving forward for the glory of God is found in John 21:18-19. Peter was willing to die on a cross if it meant that Jesus would be exalted in his life. So we need to be willing if He calls us. Willing to miss that promotion, to stick with our hard marriage, to go to that hard place, to continue to pray for and love that difficult person…we are the servants and our obedience shows our love for Him.

This is a short lesson, but now is the time to implement it! Is there anything in your life right now that makes you feel like Jonah? Like you want to run far, far away? Maybe something that the Lord was laying on your heart from yesterday's lesson? Or maybe you could just ignore the task indefinitely? Try these steps and journal what the Lord does through them below (it is not a formula, it is a heart thing). Begin taking steps of obedience during that window of time that the Holy Spirit is urging you. Be faithful to complete the task and see it through.

Lord, You do not put difficult tasks and seasons in our lives without cause. That would be contrary to Your loving nature. Only the things that will bring You the most glory will You allow and cause through Your sovereign hand. It is enjoyable and easy to submit to the blessings, we also are willing to obey You through the pain. To Whom else can we go for eternal life but You? So we will follow You as You guide us even unto death. For whoever loses their life for Your sake will find it and Your glorious presence meeting us there with power inexpressible to do Your will. For and in Jesus' name, Amen.

WEEK 6 MEMORY VERSE:

"Therefore, my dear brothers and sisters, stand firm.
Let nothing move you.
Always give yourselves fully to the work of the Lord,
because you know that your labor in the Lord is not in vain."
1 Corinthians 15:58 (NIV)

WEEK 6
DAY 4

"Better are the wounds of a friend..."

What happens when the specific thing that the Lord is telling you to do is to give someone a hard "word?" Now, some of you may be "prophets" and rebuke is your ever-loving forte (which we will address in a moment), but for some of us, it can be a right scary thing. First we waffle with the idea that we even need to say anything, then we waffle in belief of whether we heard right at all, then we move into fear of rejection and the unknown reaction that may come from the other person, then we just disobey and quench the Spirit completely! (Or at least this is my method!) I do not have all the answers, only some personal experiences that may help, along with some Scripture that will lead us through this kind of tough assignment with victory.

To start, my experience with trying to consistently walk in the Spirit, has led to many, many more words of encouragement for people than rebuke. Or, if there needed to be a word of correction, it was all sandwiched up in words of God's grace and love. Now this is when I was in the Spirit doing it! Just me, frustrated and in the flesh...not so pretty. So because God, to this day, gives words of rebuke and correction and sometimes even gives this assignment for *us* to do, we need to be prepared to obey. For people pleasers this is a hard task but we need to mature in this area so that we can be iron sharpening iron and keeping each other from falling into sin. God will give us the words to say when we need them and when we do this in love, the other person will feel it and be able to resond from their hearts and not their defenses. It may be our task to tell them, it is God's task to change them.

Please read 2 Timothy 4:1-3. What does Paul tell Timothy he is to be prepared to do "in season and out of season"?

Did you find the words "correct" and "rebuke" in there (depending on your version)? Now read the passage again to see "how" he was supposed to do this. Write the answer below.

Three quick snippits to summarize:

1. Make sure you have heard correctly. If I am supposed to do something, it is usually like a burning fire in my mind until I actually do it. I can't "shake it" and it just rolls over and over in my head (generally with specific clarification of exactly what to say and how to say it).

2. Don't delay obedience once you have prayed about it and received an answer. It will almost always keep us from following through. Go with the Spirit, when the Spirit moves, so you can complete it in the Spirit without having quenched Him.

3. Speak in love. Remember how far the Lord reached down to grab you up out of the pit. Jesus doesn't give us "words" of correction to lay condemnation down on someone. Present it in a way that they know they have the full freedom to change without our looking down our noses at them! (As though WE have never sinned or been wrong either!) The last thing anyone needs is a "know it all" shaking a finger in their face.

One thing that applies here is the principle of reaping and sowing. Specifically in this area, I find that if I am humble to *accept* rebuke and correction, I am able to correct with grace and favorable results from others. When have you ever been rebuked and how did you respond?

We need to take everything to the Lord. If we receive a hard word, don't be an island, the enemy can use that for his advantage in a big way, causing division, strife, bitterness, you name it. Run it by godly, mature Christians and get some other feedback if you don't believe what you were told lines up with reality. That is why we are to give and receive correction with meekness and humility.

Please read Proverbs 27:6. What does it say about this subject? Write this verse in your own words.

Isn't it amazing to think that if our relationships do nothing but tell each other how wonderful the other person is, without any room for correction or conflict, it is no different than what an enemy would do for us? Our skin has got to be thick enough to give and take some correction and rebuke, and I am pinching my own "thin-skin" right now! How else do we grow? It is pride that thinks we have nothing *we* need to change, and just because we have some rough edges, it doesn't mean we can't be used of God to help someone else change to be more like Him. The fine, fine line happens to be whether we do this prompted by the Spirit of God and full of His love or not.

Personally, right this minute in my own life, I have someone I need to "talk" to. This is not fun for me but I know that if I walk in the Spirit and He gives me the words to say, the proper timing, and the tone with which to say it in, it will be received (eventually!), because this person is also a Spirit-filled believer.

This aspect of hearing from God applies to our marriages, families (children and extended), friendships, and beyond. I am sure the Prophets of the Old Testament, in their flesh, did not like having to give hard words after hard words to those around them who were not following God, but it is needed to make us more like Him. We don't need to fear the hard words, we need to fear Him and obey.

Results of obeying the Lord in this area are worth it all! There is the possibility of revival breaking out in someone's heart. Or a deeper walk with the Lord and more intimacy with the other person. Healing, repentance, brokenness (in a good sense), sanctification, strength....to name a few more positive results. All God wants is our willingness to obey, He will do the rest, and I have seen beautiful things come forth from obeying God in this area. Not only from other people that He has called me to give a difficult "word" to, but also when I receive them humbly from others.

What if they do not listen? Read Jeremiah 25:7. According to this verse, to whom did they not listen, even though it was Jeremiah speaking?

What was the result of them not listening (found in the second half of this verse)?

We harm ourselves when we don't listen to the Lord, so it is in His hands. When the "word" has come out of your mouth in a Spirit-filled, godly way, your job is done. Now, your job is to stay soft and open for God to work His way in their lives and pray for them.

Here are a few verses to look at before you take this lesson and "let someone have it." First, we need to remember that we want to do unto others as we would have them do unto you. So we don't want to use an attitude or tone that we wouldn't want others to use with us.

Please read Proverbs 16:21, 24:28-29, 25:11 & 15 to name a few that will help us in this area. Jot below any thoughts you have after reading these verses.

In conclusion, I want to mention that the overarching title of week six is called "All wrapped up in love." Let this be the Spirit of everything that we do, especially in this area.

Lord, let all rebuke and correction be said, and received, in humility and love in our lives. By Your Spirit it can be so. So in Your name we pray Jesus, believing that this is Your will for us, so we will receive it from the Father. Amen.

Week 6 Memory Verse:

"Therefore, my dear brothers and sisters, stand firm.

Let nothing move you.

Always give yourselves fully to the work of the Lord,

because you know that your labor in the Lord is not in vain."

1 Corinthians 15:58 (NIV)

WEEK 6
DAY 5

"On the Brighter Side"

I thought about putting this lesson before yesterday's lesson but I thought it would be a pleasant finish for the week. This is the last day of the week "All wrapped up with Love" which is what we need to be when moving into ministry for the sake of each other. One vital aspect to this ministry is found in Proverbs 27:5. What does it say? Record it below.

Yesterday we talked about rebuke. It is not pleasant, but it can yield a peaceful fruit of righteousness when all parties involved are walking in and led by the Spirit and law of God's agape (unconditional, freeing, never ending) love. So this verse leads us to do something much more fun! It says that all the butterflies and anxieties that come with openly rebuking someone is *better* than if we conceal our love for them. So today, we are going to hear from God about who and what we need to do to openly love the people in our lives…how the Lord wants us to!

Now this can be just as difficult if we have not been practicing love in our lives. Sarcasm, complaining, biting comments, negative thoughts towards someone....these are arch-enemies of true love. If these are in place in any of our relationships, they need to be repented of (to God and the other person if appropriate, and most of the time it *is!*) and then we can be clean and able to hear and obey God for a new way to love. Is there anyone who you need to apologize to because of your lack of loving words or actions toward? God will give you the grace and strength to do this so that you can be free to love them how the Lord leads you to. Who cares what they have done to you, forgiveness is commanded of us for each other. Wipe the slate clean today and start fresh! Journal below any prayers/thoughts.

If you haven't read "The Five Love Languages" for adults and kids, no worries. The Spirit of God knows each person and how they need to be loved...and He can tell you! One way to love someone is through our words.

Please read Proverbs 15:23. Summerize it in your own words below.

Has this ever happened to you? Have you ever given or recieved a "timely word?" It is such a drink of fresh, cold water on a hot day! Just the other night, I had "had it!" For some reason, I was tired and by 9:30 p.m. the kids were not in bed because we were playing outside together (which was good), but the bedtime routine was, as you can imagine, not a pretty picture after the third glass of water (one for each kid). I was searching for a stuffed animal that hadn't been slept with in weeks, and there were giggles coming through the wall to our room after the lights were turned off. So laying in bed when the fiasco was finally over, my husband turned to me and said, "Thank you for all you do." Oh my. It was like a huge burden of "blaahhh" was lifted off my shoulders. It was a timely word, a word of love. I knew the Spirit had told him to say that because of the way it pierced right through me. But what if he had not said that? I think I would have gone to bed in my with my bedraggled attitude and probably would have had a hard time shaking it off the next morning also. Just like that, our words of love, timed by the Spirit's leading, can change others souls!

Please read Proverbs 25:11 and record what it says.

So keep our ears open (because it will come from His Spirit) to what words of love others may need to hear from us.

What does 1 John 3:18 say about openly loving someone?

It says that our lip service doesn't mean much if our actions don't back it up. What "actions" could John have been talking about?

What do you think he meant when he said to do those actions "in truth"?

I am looking forward to "hearing" this week how to love those around me better. I can't think of a better topic to end these weeks of hearing and obeying the Lord on. This is a crowning lesson and can display the love of Christ in huge ways when we seek God for ways we can lavish grace and love on each other through our words and actions.

Let's ask, *"How, Lord, can I love my family and those around me through my words and deeds? Lead me by Your Spirit as I seek to obey Your voice and feel Your power in and through my life. I want to to be confident and excited when I face You in heaven one day that I have sought and done Your will for my life in moment by moment obedience to Your leading. How we love You because You first loved us and we are forever grateful! Amen."*

WEEK 6 MEMORY VERSE:

"Therefore, my dear brothers and sisters, stand firm.
Let nothing move you.
Always give yourselves fully to the work of the Lord,
because you know that your labor in the Lord is not in vain."
1 Corinthians 15:58 (NIV)

www.ingramcontent.com/pod-product-compliance
Lightning Source LLC
LaVergne TN
LVHW081453060526
838201LV00050BA/1782